"If you build it…"

BUSINESS, GOVERNMENT, AND ONTARIO'S
ELECTRONIC TOLL HIGHWAY

BY CHANDRAN MYLVAGANAM
AND SANDFORD BORINS

To our children

Mark, Anna, and Amelia Mylvaganam

and

Alexander and Nathaniel Borins

TABLE OF CONTENTS

Canadian Cataloguing in Publication Data

Library and Archives Canada Cataloguing in Publication

Mylvaganam, Chandran, 1950-
   "If you build it... " : business, government and Ontario's
electronic toll highway / Chandran Mylvaganam and Sandford Borins.

Includes index.
ISBN 0-7727-8616-X

1. Highway 407 (Ont.) 2. Toll roads--Government policy--
Ontario--Case studies. 3. Privatization--Ontario--Case studies.
I. Borins, Sandford F., 1949- II. University of Toronto. Centre
for Public Management III. Title.

HE357.Z6O585 2004   388.1'22'09713   C2004-906662-5

Printed for the University of Toronto Centre for Public Management by
University of Toronto Press.

PREFACE

Major privatizations raise a host of Catch-22s for governments. In purely financial terms, if the enterprise to be privatized is a successful one, critics will wonder whether the government should not in fact hang on to it. If the enterprise is a troubled one, critics will home in on whether the government will possibly be able to get a good price, or strike a good deal.

In terms of the broader public interest, governments must consider how to ensure that the public values the enterprise was originally meant to serve, as a public asset, can be adequately pursued post-privatization. And yet, if the government maintains too heavy a hand, it risks undermining whatever public interest is to be served by privatization itself, as decisions that should be made on non-political criteria risk being subjected to political influence.

In attempting to negotiate these conflicting dynamics, governments have opted for any number of public-private partnership structures, some more successful than others. Rarely, though, has a case study come along of the rich sort provided by Ontario's Highway 407, in which a leading-edge toll road was initially envisaged as a public-private partnership, then developed by a special-purpose Crown corporation, and ultimately privatized by means of a multi-billion dollar 99-year lease.

The issue of road tolls is becoming an immensely significant one around the world. In technological terms, Highway 407 is, as the authors say, the "world's most technologically advanced highway" because of its integration of transponders with videoimaging. In financial terms, Highway 407 is Canada's largest privatization. And in political terms, the project had to survive a dramatic political change from an unprecedentedly (for Ontario) social-democratic government under Premier Bob Rae to an unprecedentedly free-market conservative one under Premier Mike Harris.

Chandran Mylvaganam and Sandford Borins tell a fascinating story clearly, with equal measures of rapportorial detail and analytic insight. With respect to the government's success in negotiating the public-interest

Catch-22s that such a project poses — the need to allow for not too much but not too little political direction — the authors conclude that, by and large, the Highway 407 model offers a success story for future consideration.

The Rae and Harris governments both created or adhered to institutions and structures that allowed politicians to direct the project with "passion" while keeping them "detached" from the political meddling which might otherwise have compromised the deal. The authors meticulously detail how the Crown corporation set up to oversee the project, staffed by public servants at arm's length from their home departments, and supervised by a board of external experts, managed to bring public values and private-sector insights to the process, without being tainted by either bureaucratic or business interests. Independent auditors from both the private sector, such as Price Waterhouse (as it then was), and from the public sector, in the form of the provincial auditor, provided further checks and balances.

It is when it comes to the financial and, in a particular way, the technological aspects of the 407 experience that the authors raise serious questions. Perhaps because of its ideology, the authors write, the Harris government was less likely to believe that an asset run by the public sector, or that had any governmental role in management, would be as productive or remunerative as it would be if government got out. Hence, the authors say, the Harris government allowed the purchaser an "unconscionably" long-term lease while — by focusing on its very short-term budgetary need to produce revenue for its 1999 election platform — leaving billions of dollars on the table.

Not only did the Conservatives underestimate the financial value of the highway itself, the authors claim, they passed up a valuable opportunity to create a public-private partnership to market its cutting-edge technology around the world. The Conservatives also overlooked mixed possibilities such as retaining majority governmental ownership in the Highway, but issuing shares in an IPO, thereby creating minority shareholders who would press to maximize the value of their investment. Conversely, the government failed to consider seriously how it might have retained a minority ownership stake itself so as to realize, for the public, some of the revenues ongoing, while remaining passive on managerial issues so as to allow the private owners full scope to pursue the project's financial goals unimpeded by political interference. (An example of the latter is the federal government's retaining a minority share in Petrocan which it recently sold at a highly profitable price of $65 per share, netting over $3 billion.)

The authors are uniquely placed to offer us this story. Mylvaganam was chief of staff to three transportation ministers during the Rae government, and is now a consultant and adjunct professor at Northwood University in Midland, Michigan. Borins was on the board of the Ontario Transportation Capital Corporation for three years overlapping both the Rae and Harris governments; he is professor of public management at the University of Toronto.

If You Build It... will be a valuable contribution to the growing literature on the lessons of privatization and the complexities of public-private partnership. And it is also a chapter in an ongoing story: The new Liberal government of Ontario, in seeking to veto proposed toll increases, is raising anew the question of where to draw the line between a government's legitimate role in ensuring that the public interest is served, and its own parochial interest in serving its political agenda. The latter could come at the expense of creating an environment in which potential private partners in the future will be more cautious than they ideally should be.

If You Build It... is the fourteenth monograph in the University of Toronto Centre for Public Management Monograph Series, which is funded by a generous grant from the Donner Canadian Foundation.

Andrew Stark
Editor

CHAPTER 1

PLANES, TRAINS, AND HISTORY

Like the country itself, Canada's history has been shaped by its transportation infrastructure. Railways (the Canadian Pacific, the Canadian National), airlines (Trans-Canada Airlines, later Air Canada), waterways (the St. Lawrence Seaway), and highways (the Trans-Canada) have all played central – even mythic – roles in the unfolding drama of nation-building, unifying the country's small and dispersed population across its enormous land mass.

The stories of the construction of these all-important routes have long been a part of our national romance. But the provision of this infrastructure also offers a rather different view of the building (and rebuilding) of our national identity, repeatedly raising the issue of the roles and relations of the public and private sectors in that ongoing enterprise. Simply, building transportation infrastructure requires leading-edge technology, managerial and engineering expertise, and large pools of capital. Thus, the question becomes and remains the appropriate roles of business and government in supplying each of these to any infrastructure project. Generally, the private sector would supply the technology and the expertise. A key risk in providing infrastructure is whether user-generated revenues will be sufficient to cover cost. This risk often necessitated the public sector to subsidize capital, through either grants or loan guarantees. This was demonstrated in the construction of railroads in the nineteenth century, when the public sector subsidized capital through cash and land grants (Hardin 1974, 56). The overbuilding of railroad capacity early in the twentieth century led the federal government to take over the bankrupt Canadian Northern and Grand Trunk, and consolidate them into the Canadian National Railway. Twentieth-century air transportation involved the federal government building and operating the infrastructure (airports and the air navigation system) as well as the largest carrier, Air Canada. Most of the materiel (aircraft, air traffic control technology, airport construction), however, was purchased from the private sector. Provincial governments provided highway infrastructure, with private contractors doing the construction.

The last two decades have seen the federal government divest itself of much of the transportation infrastructure for two reasons. First, the burden of deficits and a growing debt load made it attractive to sell assets and end obligations to provide operating subsidies or renew the capital stock. Second, introducing competition into the operation of both infrastructure and carriers would enhance efficiency and customer service (Advani and Borins 2001). Thus, the federal government privatized Canadian National and Air Canada, transferred the air navigation system to Nav Canada, a stakeholder-owned non-profit corporation (Mylvaganam 1997), and transferred the country's major airports to local airport authorities.

Consider Highway 407 within this historical context. For the past two hundred years, the transportation frontier was the vast space between local populations. Highway 407 is a response to the problems of a new frontier, namely the need to provide quick and uncongested transportation to residents of a densely populated urban area. There is a technological frontier here too: electronic tolling and its associated scanning and imaging capacities. The project was vast in scale and complicated in scope, encompassing the construction of over 100 kilometres of multi-lane divided highway in an urban setting and the provision of the world's most sophisticated tolling technology. Delivering the highway presented a significant challenge to its managers. The project also required raising over $1 billion in capital at a time when the Province of Ontario was running huge deficits. The project began with public sector management of private sector contractors who were building the road and supplying the tolling technology. Less than two years after the highway was opened, it had been privatized, with the right to charge tolls and obligation to provide service for 99 years sold to a private sector consortium.

Throughout its history, Highway 407 has been the source of considerable public controversy, and the controversies have all focused on different aspects of the relationship between the public and private sectors. When the winning bid to build the road was announced, irregularities in the evaluation process were alleged. In its construction phase, there were accusations that the contractors were jeopardizing safety to reduce cost. The electronic toll system became operational several months after the road itself opened, leading to criticisms of the government's effectiveness at contracting for and managing technology. Privatization has led to criticisms that the Harris government acted too hastily and failed to protect the public interest. Critics have also claimed that the private sector owners are offering poor service – for example, in their billing practices – while charging rapacious tolls. The McGuinty government, elected in October 2003, has interpreted the privatization agreement differently than its predecessor, asserting that the agreement gives it a veto over toll increases.

This book has two objectives: documentation and evaluation. We will chart the history of Highway 407, from its development to its privatization, as well as its performance since. We will also assess the project, determining the validity of the various criticisms leveled against it. We will identify successful aspects to be emulated, and failures to be avoided. The implications of our findings extend beyond the highway itself to issues such as the management of technology projects, urban transportation policy, and the relationship between the public and private sectors.

While the public controversy surrounding Highway 407 has generated many debates in the Ontario Legislature as well as significant media attention, it has not yet been studied in a scholarly and comprehensive way.[1] There have been two studies to date, and their conclusions are conflicting. The Canadian Council for Public-Private Partnerships (2000) gave Highway 407 its gold award for financial partnerships. Joan Boase (1999) mentioned Highway 407 in an article in *Canadian Public Administration* comparing several private-public partnerships. She came down firmly in the critics' camp, citing cost overruns and delays implementing the technology, the assumption of the entire risk for the project by the Ontario taxpayer, and what she claimed was an absence of democratic accountability.

Our study will provide a more comprehensive perspective on Highway 407 than either of its predecessors. We recount the highway's history in some detail, calling upon not only public sources such as newspaper articles, legislative debates, and the Provincial Auditor's reports, but also the authors' experiences as inside observers of the decision-making process. Chandran Mylvaganam was chief of staff to the Ontario Minister of Transportation from 1990 to 1995 and an adviser to one of the unsuccessful bidders when the highway was privatized; Sandford Borins was a member of the board of directors of the Ontario Transportation Capital Corporation, the Crown corporation responsible for building the highway, from 1995 to 1998. We describe ourselves as observers because neither was a key decision-maker, but we were reasonably close to the thinking of those who were. We have also interviewed many senior public servants associated with the management of the project. Some of those we have interviewed have also commented on drafts of this book.

We begin with a discussion of the background to Highway 407 in terms of economic growth in the Greater Toronto Area (GTA). Chapter 3 then describes the Ministry of Transportation's standard approach to highway construction, and why it was inappropriate in this instance, outlining how the financial constraints of the recession of the early Nineties led the Rae government to develop this highway by seeking out private sector partnerships and using leading-edge electronic road pricing technology. Chapter 4 describes how the Rae government implemented this new approach to highway development by establishing a process for two private sector consortia to bid on constructing the road, installing the road-pricing technology, and financing the project. Chapter 5 discusses the government's choice of a consortium to build the highway as well as the controversy that the decision created.

While the method of contracting was itself unconventional, the method of monitoring the contract was no less a departure from tradition. Chapter 6 discusses the establishment, functions, and staffing of the Ontario Transportation Capital Corporation, a Crown corporation with the responsibility for overseeing both road construction and development of the electronic tolling system. The chapter also discusses the approach taken to funding the highway. Chapter 7 deals with the building of the highway, in particular, crises that occurred when the road design was criticized as unsafe and the tolling technology was not working. The chapter culminates with the resolution of these crises and the opening of Highway 407 as an electronic toll road. Traffic grew rapidly, and approximately two years after its opening, Highway 407 was privatized; chapter 8 deals with the process and the choice of a consortium to hold a 99-year lease on the highway. Though the privatization maximized immediate revenue to the government, we argue that this was not in the long-term public interest. The chapter also discusses developments after privatization, including the McGuinty government's ongoing dispute with the concessionaire.

Chapter 9 represents our final evaluation of Highway 407 from several points of view. We look at its performance as a large technology-based project and we consider the effectiveness of OTCC as an organizational structure for managing such projects. We discuss the significance of political and bureaucratic leadership in implementing the 407 project. We review the fairness and transparency of the development and privatization processes and assess the appropriateness of tolls charged. We propose two alternative models of operating Highway 407 that would have been more consistent with the public interest. Finally, as a means of placing this single, complex case in a larger theoretical context, we address the key issues of public management and transportation policy it raises and draw out lessons.

Following chapter 9, we have included a chronological appendix for the reader's reference.

CHAPTER 2

THE 401 PARKING LOT AND THE BIRTH OF
HIGHWAY 407

In the late 1950s, the Ontario government embarked on an ambitious program of freeway planning and construction, resulting in the 400 series of multi-lane controlled access highways. In that exercise, it identified the possible future need for a highway in the Toronto region to run in a more or less east-west direction and north of the soon-to-be-constructed Highway 401. This planned highway was designated as Highway 407. In the 1950s, the necessary corridor was identified as a part of the Parkway Belt lands and property acquisition to safeguard it began. Most of the property required for the highway's right of way, with the exception of a few small sections in Mississauga to the west, was assembled in the 1950s. Environmental approvals were also secured east to Highway 48 (Markham Road).

As development grew around the Greater Toronto area, the area north of Highway 401, which had been farmland in the 1960s, was turned into residential sub-divisions. Small towns north of Toronto, like Markham and Newmarket, became busy bedroom communities. Traffic volumes grew. The section of Highway 401 that ran through the Toronto area became one of the two busiest stretches of road in North America, competing for that distinction with Southern California's Santa Monica Freeway.

Industrial policy plays a role in highway planning. Highways are acknowledged to be economic generators, bringing development and industry to their corridors and the surrounding areas. The 401 corridor near Toronto had been an unmitigated success in this respect. Numerous industries had located along this corridor because of the ready highway access to major markets and industrial centres in Canada and the northern United States. This was particularly true of the automotive sector, which was the largest industry in Ontario and was vital to the strength of the province's economy. The highway corridor, from the General Motors complex in Oshawa to the Chrysler plants in Windsor, was studded with manufacturing plants and suppliers to this industry in Canada and the United States. As on-site inventories were minimized and just-in-time deliveries became more critical to this industry, fast transportation links grew in importance. Trucking became a de facto part of the assembly line. Unimpeded flow of traffic on the 401 was crucial to the automobile industry and consequentially to the Ontario economy. This was illustrated vividly in 1989 and 1990 when disaffected owner-operators used their rigs to block the highway. The "big three" automakers let the government know that this shutdown of their "assembly line" would force plants to cease operations very quickly. The government immediately negotiated with the drivers to lift the blockades and avert the plant closings and potential economic fallout.

Growth of the communities north of the 401, however, increased traffic congestion significantly. This, in turn, raised concerns of negative economic impacts well beyond commuter rush-hour aggravation. Truckers claimed that congestion added three hours to their business, effectively adding to the cost of manufacturing an automobile. An internal Ministry of Transportation (MTO) study in the 1980s estimated that congestion in the Greater Toronto Area (GTA) cost Ontario's commercial and industrial sectors $2 billion annually as a result of lost productivity and delayed shipments. An MTO survey of truckers from Northern Ontario identified congestion on the 401 in the Greater Toronto Area as their biggest concern, ahead of factors such as poor road conditions or higher fuel prices in the north. There were growing calls to increase highway capacity in the GTA to ease this congestion.[1]

The Ontario government responded to these concerns by adding lanes to the 401. This was considered a short-term fix by MTO staff, who favoured commencing construction of the 407. The cost of a new four-lane highway, however, estimated at approximately $20 million per kilometre, was a strong deterrent to the government.

In the late 1980s the Ontario economy was booming, leading to even greater congestion on the 401. In the area north of Toronto, the state of the highway had become an election issue. In 1986, then Deputy Minister of Transportation, David Hobbs, took Premier David Peterson on a helicopter flight during rush hour to provide a bird's eye view of what was sometimes referred to as the "401 parking lot". Shortly after that flight, the government announced that it would proceed with Highway 407 between Highway 410 and Highway 48, a 69-kilometre section. A groundbreaking ceremony took place just before the 1987 provincial election. One of the gold painted shovels used in the ceremony was placed on prominent display in the boardroom of the Minister of Transportation, where it hung for several years, even after the government changed in 1990.

CHAPTER 3

FROM CRISIS TO INNOVATION

This chapter describes the Ontario Government's traditional approaches to capital budgeting and awarding highway construction contracts. The rationale for building the 407 as a toll highway and utilizing an all-electronic tolling system is discussed.

CAPITAL BUDGETING

The Ministry of Transportation is responsible for building and maintaining provincial highways as well as, until 1998, sharing the cost of roads and bridges in the more than 800 municipalities in Ontario. In the early 1990s, it had the largest capital budget within the government, totaling approximately $1.9 billion. Of this figure, $1.5 billion was for provincial and municipal roads, with the remaining $400 million for transit. The demands of the province's road system, however, had consistently outstripped the availability of funds for several years. Ontario's highway system, which had expanded rapidly in the 1950s and 60s, was reaching a stage where major rebuilding was required. Highway maintenance had been sacrificed in previous years to divert funds to build or expand new highways. These roads were sometimes of questionable economic utility, but frequently of political significance. While new highways were clearly needed to meet the needs of the growing population, a kilometre of new four-lane expressway was estimated to cost approximately $20 million. By the early 1990s, all the ingredients of a crisis were present: a worsening, highly visible problem, and a prohibitively expensive solution.

Highway construction, like all other capital spending by the province, is financed from general revenues. The process begins with MTO staff ranking projects for the coming fiscal year. Priority was determined by a needs assessment, taking into consideration factors such as road condition, condition of bridges and other structures, traffic volumes, accident rates, and economic development imperatives. An attempt was made to provide some regional balance to the list. If purely objective criteria such as traffic volumes, economic importance, and even accident rates were the sole determinants, very few projects outside the Golden Horseshoe (the conurbation stretching around the western end of Lake Ontario from Oshawa through Toronto to Niagara Falls) would be built. (This came as a surprise to many irate telephone callers to the minister's office who were convinced that if only these above-mentioned objective criteria applied, projects in Toronto would be halted in favour of those in their regions.) The Ministry of Northern Development participated fully in decision making about the northern highways program. Political input was often provided at this stage by the minister's staff, who would identify projects of interest to the minister or key legislators.

A list of projects would be drawn up, based on this staff ranking and on the budget that Treasury staff had informally told MTO it could expect to receive. The projects, which included higher cost maintenance-type projects, such as the rebuilding of road beds, as well as new highway and bridge construction would be presented to the Minister for approval. (The Minister of Northern Development also had to approve the Northern highways program.) At this stage, political considerations could again come into play. A project of importance to a government legislator could be included, even though it had not received a high priority from staff. After the minister had signed off on the list, it had to be approved by the Management Board of Cabinet and, finally, by the cabinet as a whole.

Since the budget allocation was an annual exercise, project funding was also committed on an annual basis only. Theoretically, large projects, which could take several years to complete, could only have funds committed on a year-to-year basis, with no guarantee that funds would be available the following year to continue the work. The level of funds available each year formed a further constraint. Construction of a large project such as Highway 407 would have to be spread out over several years, because only a limited amount of funds could be allocated annually. Any larger allocation would have resulted in other projects around the province not proceeding.

Politically this was unacceptable. No government could afford to sacrifice projects in other regions of the province for the benefit of a single mega-project in the Toronto area. Practically, too, concentration of resources could not be permitted since much necessary maintenance and repair still had to be carried out simply to arrest the deterioration of the highway system.

HIGHWAY CONSTRUCTION CONTRACTS

Since the 1950s, MTO had followed a rigorous process when awarding contracts for highway construction. Ministry staff precisely defined parcels of work and sealed bids were accepted from contractors who were deemed to be qualified on the basis of financial soundness and demonstrated competence. Contractors were permitted to bid on projects up to their level of financial qualification. Since there was no differentiation in design or construction quality, price was the only selection criterion and the lowest bidder was awarded the contract. The road construction industry was heavily dependent on work from MTO and from municipalities. Since municipalities received a large part of their capital funding from MTO, particularly for major projects, they were required to adhere to MTO's standards.

MTO staff supervised construction closely to ensure that the contractor was strictly adhering to all technical requirements of the job. Process specifications were prevalent; there were few end-product specifications. In other words, the ministry kept a close eye on how the project was being delivered, but it did not ask for performance guarantees on particulars, for example, the integrity of the road surface over a specified time frame. As a result, the highway contractors needed to concern themselves with construction efficiency alone. They did not have to develop new expertise in highway construction methods, as this was effectively done for them by MTO. The system allowed a number of smaller companies to exist around the province, bidding exclusively on projects in their home regions.

The result was a flourishing Ontario road construction industry, with firms ranging in size from numerous small contractors bidding on jobs of a few hundred thousand dollars or less, to a few large companies capable of handling projects worth tens of million dollars, though projects of this size were few and far between.

MTO's system of parceling out even large projects into bite-sized pieces suited the industry. There was sufficient work every year for smaller members. Projects were spread around the province, giving companies in all regions a chance to bid on contracts. A handful of larger projects kept the bigger contractors busy. The system was free of taint, but not very efficient. Parceling out projects in small increments limited the ability to reap economies of scale. It did, however, serve the political needs of the Conservatives who had instituted the system and who counted small road builders throughout the province among their supporters.

After the Liberals succeeded the Conservatives as the government in 1985, some overzealous political staff apparently attempted to tap into this source of support. Successful bidders for highway contracts began receiving letters soliciting political donations soon after they were notified by MTO of the contract award. The linkage was unmistakable. The Deputy Minister of Transportation learned that the Minister's staff were participants in this exercise and informed the Premier's office, which put a stop to the practice.

The contracts for Highway 407 were a part of this routine tendering process and were let in a similar manner. Each year a finite amount of funding was made available for contracts related to Highway 407 from MTO's capital budget. As a result, the highway proceeded piecemeal and completion of the first 69-kilometre section was expected around the year 2020, based on the rate at which it was being funded to that point.

In September 1990, Bob Rae's New Democrats defeated the Liberal government led by David Peterson. The Rae government advocated a strategy of reducing the cost of government by delivering services more efficiently. In the case of road building, this meant having larger work packages and using the expertise of the private sector in contracts involving both design and building. Clearly, this would give larger companies a material advantage. Deprived of the government hand-holding to which they were accustomed, some of the smaller road builders would not be able to survive. Since the Rae government did not have close political ties to the road building industry, ensuring the survival of smaller contractors was not an issue of political concern.

There was a concern, however, over external competition. As the U.S. – Canada free trade agreement and NAFTA opened up the North American market, there were fears that large American road builders with long experience operating in a design/build environment would dominate the Ontario market before the domestic industry had an opportunity to reconfigure itself. The government therefore actively sought some large design/build projects to give the Ontario industry experience in this kind of environment. (In hindsight this concern was misplaced, as the feared "invasion" has not yet taken place. A few foreign-owned road builders operate in Ontario, but ironically, many of them are here as a result of the 1999 privatization of Highway 407.)

THE RECESSION

Soon after taking office in September 1990, the Rae government was faced with the effects of the deepest recession to hit the province since the 1930s. It attempted to alleviate the effects of the recession with a limited program of government-funded capital projects, the "Anti-Recession Program." This proved sadly inadequate as, contrary to most forecasts, the recession showed few signs of disappearing. Unemployment grew and as the surge of construction in the commercial sector from the 1980s all but disappeared, construction-related employment dropped. With declining revenues and ballooning social assistance payments, the budget deficit grew. This limited the ability of the government to stimulate the economy with more interventionist expenditures. Inside the government there was growing talk of hitting a "borrowing wall," where the province's debt rating would be downgraded to the point where it would become prohibitively expensive to borrow to finance its activities. The search began for creative methods of economic stimulus and job creation that would not contribute to the deficit.

EFFICIENT UTILIZATION OF CAPITAL

Budgetary constraints also gave rise to concerns about expenditures on long-term projects. The government was acutely aware that at a time of fiscal constraint scarce capital dollars were being spent with no return in the foreseeable future. Highway 407, which was not expected to be completed until 2020, fell into this category. The most glaring example of such spending was the interchange between Highways 407 and 400 that had been built in 1989 at a cost of approximately $50 million. This interchange would not be used for several more years. Meanwhile, carrying costs continued to mount on the original capital expenditure, with no benefit of usage. The government asked the ministry to find a more efficient way of completing large capital projects.

OFF-BOOK FINANCING

There was a strong sentiment within the political leadership of the government that the current method of budgeting did not give a realistic picture of the province's financial state and greatly overstated the size of the deficit. It was felt that the provincial budget should be divided into separate operating and capital components. The theory was that current revenues should cover operating costs, while borrowing, with carrying costs covered by revenues, could reasonably cover capital costs. The analogy often used by both the Premier and the Minister of Transportation, Gilles Pouliot, was the difference between buying groceries and buying a house with a mortgage. You should pay for your groceries from your current income and not go into debt to finance them. It was perfectly acceptable to go into debt to buy a house, however, as long as you could make your mortgage payments from current income. Instituting this new form of budgeting would be a major departure from past practice and was certain to meet with criticism. The government therefore looked for alternate ways in which it could implement this, such as moving capital projects out of the annual budget.

THE ENGINEERING INDUSTRY AND DESIGN/BUILD

By the early 1990s, the consulting engineering community in Ontario had been actively pursuing international projects for several years and had enjoyed some success. Members of the community had been concerned for some time, however, over an increasing competitive disadvantage in the perception of their experience. Competitors, such as those from Quebec, had managed the entire design and construction of mega-projects. Quebec in particular had used the construction of Hydro Quebec facilities in that province to develop its consulting engineering industry, which was thus able to point to these mega-projects as demonstrations of their expertise.

Ontario firms, however, had access in their home base only to smaller projects, such as those of the Ministry of Transportation. When the Ministry of Transportation built a new road, it maintained close control of the process. The project, including highway design and structures, was broken into discrete work packages. It was these smaller design engineering packages that were usually contracted out to a consulting engineering firm. Ontario Hydro, the other big developer of capital works in Ontario, did the bulk of its own engineering and managed its own projects. There was little opportunity for consulting engineers to obtain significant work there either.

Ontario engineers, particularly the larger firms, asked the government to change its approach and launch some larger design-build projects that they could then showcase when competing for external work. They lobbied the Ministry of Industry Trade and Technology, a policy-making ministry, as well as MTO, the Ministry of Municipal Affairs and Housing and the Ministry of the Environment, the biggest procurers of design engineering and construction services. They also made the same argument to the Premier's office, with some effect. Mylvaganam, who had previously worked at Ontario Hydro, recalls a conversation he had in 1991 with David Agnew, then the Premier's Principal Secretary and later Secretary to the Cabinet. In that discussion, Agnew spoke very favourably about the approach Hydro Quebec had taken to develop the Quebec-based engineering industry and was critical of Ontario Hydro for doing most of its work in-house, precluding a similar development in Ontario.

The consulting engineers Marshall Macklin Monaghan (MMM) were particularly active in lobbying. MMM had managed the design-build process for Terminal 3 at Toronto's Pearson Airport. Because of the design-build nature of the project, construction could be commenced while elements of the detailed design were still in progress. Since they were held only to end-product specifications, they were unrestricted by government-specified construction processes, and were able to innovate in this area as well. As a result, Terminal 3 was completed in less than half the time and a fraction of the cost that Transport Canada had originally anticipated for a new terminal, according to Transport Canada staff who were on the site. (It should be noted that not everyone at Transport Canada publicly subscribes to this view.) MMM had leveraged this experience to obtain airport design contracts and had become one of the leading firms in this area internationally. They made the argument that more large design/build projects by the Ontario government would bring a similar measure of success in other areas for the consulting industry.

ROAD PRICING AND MTO

Independently of the government's fiscal pressures in the early 1990s, MTO had begun intensive study of alternate ways of paying for transportation infrastructure, such as private sector investment and road pricing, both used in other jurisdictions. A new position of Director of Investment Strategy was created in January 1992. Tony Salerno, a long-time Ontario Public Service (OPS) employee, with previous experience at MTO and Treasury, was appointed to this position. His mandate was to devise ways in which external investment, including direct and indirect third-party participation, could be made in Ontario's transportation infrastructure.

Large-scale construction of new toll routes in Western European countries such as France, Spain and Italy, had been undertaken in recent years, as well as a more limited program in parts of the United States. This model – making users of a highway pay directly for the facility – was attractive to the ministry, which felt that it was never allocated sufficient funds to meet its construction and maintenance needs.

MTO staff realized, however, that there would be political obstacles to instituting any form of road pricing (or toll roads) in Ontario. Ontarians were simply no longer accustomed to paying tolls. The last toll facility in Ontario, the Burlington Skyway bridge, had tolls removed in 1973, because the cost of collection was greater than the toll receipts. This was a result both of low toll rates and what was euphemistically referred to as "leakage" of toll revenues at the point of collection. MTO staff also had a strong suspicion that while the Treasury probably would not object to tolling roads, or indeed any other facility, all revenues would flow into the consolidated revenue fund, and MTO would have to continue to rely on annual allocations from the Treasury to finance highway construction.

In early 1992, the Premier's office asked MTO to determine the feasibility of instituting alternate methods for the provision of transportation infrastructure that did not rely on financing from the provincial budget. The Premier's office also specifically asked whether a tolled 407 was viable.

THE DISCUSSION PAPER

In June 1992, MTO produced a discussion paper on alternative methods of providing transportation infrastructure. The paper concluded that models for financing and building highways based on dedicated revenues that underwrote long-term debt financing were viable. It proposed, too, that such methods could significantly reduce actual construction time and cost. These conclusions were based on experience in Europe and the United States. The paper was generic in its approach and did not explicitly discuss Highway 407. It was the sense of all participants, however, that Highway 407 would be the first facility to be handled in such a manner, if the government decided to proceed.

Surveys showed that there was strong public acceptance of tolls and a capital corporation to administer the scheme, if the tolls were dedicated to funding the facility, and if the facility were unlikely to be built otherwise. There were other public policy benefits from tolling, as it provided a tool for controlling the level of traffic using the facility. The paper also suggested that a key principle of social equity when tolling highways was that an alternate free route should always be available. Interestingly, the paper assumed that tolls were unlikely to cover the entire cost of capital, though they would make a significant contribution to the capital cost.

One of the factors that made it possible to toll an urban highway like 407 was the availability of new electronic tolling technologies that lessened the need for traditional tollbooths. Tollbooths at all entrances and exits would have been impractical for an urban expressway that would have required these at intervals of several kilometres at most.

Highway 407, then, appeared to be suitable for the approach outlined in the discussion paper. Because construction had already begun, however, the paper recommended that questions regarding operations and safety necessitated further study. These reservations, as well as concern about recovering the entire cost of capital, were considered typical of the rather conservative character of MTO. After some discussion between the deputy minister of transportation, the minister, and the premier's policy advisers, MTO was directed to proceed with development of a plan to accelerate construction of Highway 407 as a toll road, using dedicated financing.

"IF YOU BUILD IT...."

Transportation Minister Gilles Pouliot represented the Northern Ontario riding of Lake Nipigon, which, he was fond of saying, was the size of (the former) West Germany. Like most northern members of the Legislature, he spent much of his time at Queen's Park trying to obtain adequate infrastructure and services for his vast, but under-populated region. It was inconceivable to him that, given the congestion on the 401, users would not flock to the 407, making it fully self-financing. A baseball fan, he often quoted a modified version of the signature line from the novel Shoeless Joe to illustrate his view: "If you build it, they will come."[1] Despite his certainty, he felt impelled to defer to the expertise of the MTO staff who were more cautious. More thorough studies would later show that Pouliot's instincts were correct and that Highway 407 could indeed be entirely self-financing.

CHAPTER 4

DELIVERING THE INNOVATION

INTRODUCTION

By late 1992, the Rae government had a sense of the broad directions for the development of Highway 407. The highway the government envisioned would be innovative in three ways. First, in response to the severity of both the recession and traffic congestion in the GTA, it was to be built much faster than traditional practice would dictate. Second, rather than parceling the project out bit-by-bit to small contractors, the government would invite larger firms and/or consortia to make proposals to design and build the entire highway. Third, in response to the government's fiscal crisis, the highway would be financed by tolls collected electronically.[1]

When an organization attempts to introduce an innovation, it will likely face some predictable obstacles (Borins 1998, 66-91; 2001, 8-26). Highway 407 could be expected to incur the opposition of the MTO bureaucracy, because it represented an implicit critique of their practices and raised the possibility of removing the most significant highway project in decades from their control. The highway depended on a new technology that seemed fine in concept but would have to be implemented. Outsourcing the design and construction of the highway in one major contract meant that there would have to be a competition that could have only one winner. The government would have to demonstrate, to the satisfaction of both the general public and the loser(s) in the competition, that the process had been fair. Finally, there were numerous stakeholders whose interests would be affected by any new highway, and especially a toll road. These included municipalities, the trucking industry, drivers, road builders, organized labour, environmentalists, and the New Democratic Party. The government would have to win their support at the outset, or overcome their opposition later on.

This chapter tells the story of how the government moved forward on delivering its innovation by coping with all these sources of potential opposition. We first deal with the organizational context. We then outline the steps taken to win stakeholder support. We next describe the contracting process, starting from the development of an action plan, to the choice of two contractors to bid on the project, the bids themselves, and the evaluation of the bids. Given the magnitude of the project and the innovations involved, the process was adaptive, in the sense that participants were learning by doing, and as a consequence, plans were revised and decisions modified in the light of additional information.

This part of the story begins in February 1993, when Premier Rae publicly announced that Highway 407 would be accelerated from its current schedule and would be constructed as a toll facility. He invited the private sector to participate or to partner with the government, as the province would entertain new ways of constructing this highway. He felt strongly that private sector involvement would lead to innovation and efficiencies that were less likely with the status quo.

THE ORGANIZATIONAL CONTEXT

The government took a number of steps to create the organizational capacity to manage the contracting process. First and foremost, a new deputy minister of transportation was appointed. A structure for inter-ministerial collaboration was created and consultants were hired. The process was also structured to minimize political involvement in decision-making about the contract. This section deals with two additional aspects of the project's development within MTO, the process of consultation between the minister and the department, and dissatisfaction within the department about the decision to outsource a major contract.

A new deputy minister of transportation

One of the powers of a premier is the appointment of deputy ministers. Deputy ministers serve as a government's senior management team, and a premier will organize the team to bring particular strengths to bear on certain issues. In January 1993, Premier Rae announced an extensive reassignment of deputy ministers as well as a number of retirements. One of the retirements was Gary Posen, the deputy minister of transportation. Premier Rae wanted to see progress on two key transportation priorities – Highway 407 and four additional subway lines in Toronto – and he wanted a deputy minister who would provide strong and energetic leadership, with a commitment to delivering results quickly. He chose George Davies, who had previously been

Deputy Minister of Energy, and had acquired a reputation as a hard-driving, results-oriented executive, willing to challenge his staff and bruise egos in his quest for results.

Davies' first moves regarding Highway 407 displayed his "take charge" attitude. A few days after Davies' arrival, MTO was scheduled to report to the Policy and Priorities Board of Cabinet – Cabinet's key strategy and policy-setting committee, chaired by Premier Rae – on progress made in developing a strategy for financing and constructing Highway 407 as a toll facility. In fact, Posen, who had just retired as deputy minister, also attended the meeting because of his familiarity with the file. MTO's Quality and Standards Division was very cautious in its prediction of traffic on the new highway, claiming that while a toll highway was technically feasible, tolls would cover only 30 % of the capital costs of the highway. The Ministry of Finance had been strongly supportive of proceeding with a toll highway, because it would not place demands on the provincial treasury. It was concerned that the MTO study was overly conservative and could potentially derail the option of a toll highway. Shortly before the Policy and Priorities Board (P&P) meeting, Davies had been alerted that the Ministry of Finance believed the MTO presentation, to be made by Margaret Kelch, Assistant Deputy Minister for Quality and Standards, would be overly cautious. Furthermore, it was made clear to Davies that if MTO did not pursue the project more energetically, the leading role would be given to another ministry. When Kelch completed her presentation to P&P, Davies explicitly undercut it, hastily interjecting that "there are differing views within the ministry." He undertook to commission an extensive review of toll road experience. This task was handed to the Policy and Planning Division of the ministry, led by Assistant Deputy Minister David Guscott, who shortly reported back to Davies that the toll highway could be self-financing.

Consultation between the minister and the department

Well before Davies' arrival at MTO, Minister Pouliot and senior staff had devised a streamlined policy development and decision-making structure. The minister's staff, headed by Chandran Mylvaganam, who had been at MTO with Pouliot's predecessor, had established close working relations with the civil service. A degree of mutual trust had developed and the civil servants used the staff as a sounding board to get a sense of the minister's thinking. Minister's staff were also able to discuss issues informally with the minister and provide feedback to the civil servants about possible areas of concern. The deputy minister and his senior staff would then develop policy alternatives. After additional informal discussion with Mylvaganam, the alternatives were presented to Minister Pouliot with recommendations. Because of the magnitude of the 407 project, the minister's preferred alternative, which was usually the recommendation of the ministry, would also be discussed with the Premier's policy advisers and their concurrence sought. In all instances, they agreed with the minister's preferences. At certain critical decision points, P&P was also asked to approve proposed steps or to provide guidance as to which of various alternatives should be chosen. All the minister's decisions were accepted by P&P.

Dissatisfaction within MTO

MTO had traditionally regarded itself as a builder of highways. In recent years, however, governments had attempted to change that view by transforming it into a transportation ministry responsible for the movement of goods and people, increasing its role in transit as well. Inside MTO, the focus had remained on building roads and bridges, with the funding of transit services viewed almost as an add-on. The Rae government, as a part of its overall government reform strategy, wanted to carry the transformation further, re-making MTO as an economic development ministry. Economic development considerations were to be given greater weight when priorities were set, whether for roads or transit. Ministry staff, who were justifiably proud of their record in fulfilling the original mandate of highway construction, felt that their world was in turmoil, as new deputy ministers who came from outside the ministry reorganized it to deliver on the new mandates.

Until the mid-1980s, the deputy minister of transportation had always been an engineer who had spent virtually his entire career within the ministry. Since then, only non-engineers had held this position, to the discomfort of the managers and professionals in the ministry, the bulk of whom were engineers. Davies, an economist, often quipped that he too was an engineer – "a social engineer"! Staff in MTO were not amused, or mollified.

Regarding the new method of delivering Highway 407, therefore, the reaction within MTO was not, on the whole, positive. The senior executive of the ministry, led by Davies, enthusiastically supported the project. The many staff who would have been involved in the project had it been delivered in the traditional manner, with tight MTO controls, felt resentful that a project of this magnitude had been taken away from them. They interpreted public pronouncements by the Premier and the Minister about harnessing the energies and abilities of the private sector as an implicit criticism of their own lack of creativity and innovative potential. They viewed the new approach to Highway 407 as reinforcement of the message that the way they had done things in the past needed to be reformed. The question that naturally arises is whether their quiet resentment would give rise to covert opposition.

Interministerial decision-making and external advisers

Outsourcing so important a project had implications for the entire government, with the consequence that the planning process had to move beyond MTO. An inter-ministerial team, the Highway 407 inter-ministerial committee, was created in March 1993 to manage the process. George Davies had reasserted MTO's commitment to the project, so MTO took the lead, supported by Finance, Treasury Board, Cabinet Office, and the Ministry of Economic Development and Trade (MEDT). Recognizing the limitations of the government's financial expertise regarding the private sector, Goldman Sachs and CIBC Wood Gundy were retained as financial advisers. Other external advisers and consultants were to be retained as necessary. The first was Wilbur Smith Associates (WSA), an American company with an international reputation for expertise in developing traffic and revenue forecasts. IBI Consultants, an Ontario firm, was retained to work alongside them to enable development of Ontario expertise in this field. Price Waterhouse was brought in to advise on managing the process.

Minimizing political involvement

In opposition, the NDP had been harshly critical of Conservative and Liberal governments for allegedly favouring supporters when awarding government contracts. Most recently, it had witnessed the controversies surrounding the redevelopment of Terminals 1 and 2 at Toronto's Pearson International Airport, as well as the construction of the Confederation Bridge to Prince Edward Island by the Mulroney government. Both projects had engendered widespread belief that lobbyists for the successful proponents, with close ties to the government, had used their access to members of the government and their staffs to improperly influence the design of the process and the evaluation of the tenders. (Indeed, the controversy grew so intense that the Liberals, who defeated the Conservatives later in 1993, cancelled the Pearson contract.)

From the outset, therefore, the Rae government wanted to ensure that the process surrounding Highway 407 be perceived as fair and untainted. It drew a clear line barring any involvement by members of the government, or their political staff, in the evaluation of the proposals. While P&P and Cabinet approved the contracting process and made policy decisions, at no time were any members of the political side of the government involved in or consulted on the evaluation of the proposals.

When P&P decided in April 1993 to proceed with the project, Premier Rae cautioned all those present against any interaction with members of the consortia who would be bidding on the project (or the lobbyists they would undoubtedly hire) that could in any way be construed as improper. As he put it, he did not want anyone involved in the process, including ministers and their staff to have as much as a cup of coffee with any of the bidders or their representatives.

GETTING STAKEHOLDERS ON BOARD

The government engaged in a process of consultation with the affected interest groups throughout the planning process. This consultation took the form of opinion surveys, focus groups, and contacts with interest group leaders. Results revealed general support for accelerating the construction of Highway 407 and levying tolls to pay for it, provided tolls were removed once the highway had been paid for.

Elected local officials, such as mayors and regional chairs of the municipalities through which the highway would run, were kept informed about the process. They were strongly supportive of a project that they felt would alleviate some of the traffic congestion in their regions and also spur development. There were some issues of specifically local concern. The planned route of a proposed link road between Highways 407 and 401 in the Durham region generated some opposition in Whitby. Since this was not a part of the immediate project, it did not give the government much immediate concern, though two government MPPs from the region were on opposite sides of the issue.

Business groups, such as Boards of Trade and Chambers of Commerce, strongly supported acceleration of the highway, which they viewed as essential to relieve congestion and speed east-west traffic flow in the GTA north of Toronto. They accepted tolls as a necessary cost to accomplish this.

The Ontario Road Builders Association welcomed acceleration of the highway, but was concerned that a big design-build contract would exclude smaller firms. The association asked the government to ensure that these smaller contractors would have an opportunity to participate. The government did not make any commitments, but in various responses implied that smaller contractors would be able to sub-contract work from the larger direct participants in the project.

The government was concerned that user groups, such as the Ontario Trucking Association, the Canadian Automobile Association and the Ontario Motor Coach Association, would oppose the levying of tolls. Support for the acceleration of construction was unanimous, however, with tolls accepted as a necessary means to this end. An often-voiced reservation was that the government took more money from road users in the form of fees and taxes than it put into highway construction and maintenance. User groups did argue strongly that tolls should be removed once the highway had been paid for and were also insistent that toll rates should not be excessive.

Organized labour strongly supported the project. They viewed it as a major generator of jobs for the slumping construction industry. Construction unions such as the Labourers, Carpenters, Operating Engineers and Teamsters would regularly contact members of the government and the minister's staff to say how much they wanted the project to proceed. Before the Premier made his announcement in February 1993, they would also privately express their concern that it was being stalled in the bureaucracy.

The government feared that environmental groups, who were one of its strongest constituencies, would oppose acceleration of the highway. This opposition did not materialize for several reasons. They reluctantly accepted that Highway 407, which was already under way, would be completed at some point, so acceleration per se was not a major issue. What is more, they strongly supported tolling the highway as a way of deterring usage and hence decreasing pollution. The government had already earned a measure of "green" credibility through a series of pro-environmental actions. Even MTO, which was not generally viewed by the environmental community as being particularly enviro-friendly, had, in one of the Rae government's first acts, withdrawn funding for the controversial Red Hill Creek Expressway in Hamilton on environmental grounds. As a consequence, environmentalists were disposed to give the government the benefit of the doubt and accept assurances that it would take all necessary measures to mitigate the environmental impacts of the highway. There were also some specific issues that were raised and addressed. For instance, a culvert had originally been planned for the crossing of the East Don river. After environmental organizations met with the minister, it was decided to replace this with a more expensive three-span bridge, which would have less impact on the environment.

Support for the project had to be cultivated within the NDP. Highway construction was not popular among many party members who felt that transportation policy should be skewed towards development of transit. This was balanced, however, by the job creation benefits of construction. While tolls had environmental benefits, they also smacked of fostering social inequity. Mylvaganam heard unhappy comments from some of his counterparts in other ministries about the rich being able to ride in uncongested comfort on toll highways, while the average motorist had to make do with the stop and go traffic on Highway 401. Rae and Pouliot actively addressed these concerns by making the case for tolling and accelerating Highway 407 at NDP gatherings. Overt opposition soon dissipated.

Members of the legislature who were affected by the highway, as well as the opposition parties' transportation critics, were regularly briefed on the progress of the project. MPPs in the affected ridings, many of whom were members of the opposition parties, supported accelerating the highway and financing it by tolls. In the absence of significant criticism by interest groups, neither the Liberals nor the Conservatives saw any political benefit in opposing the concept of tolling Highway 407. The Conservatives did voice the concern that smaller road builders would be shut out of the process.

PRIVATE SECTOR INTEREST

A consortium named the Ontario Road Development Corporation (ORDC) had been formed some months before Premier Rae's announcement. It consisted of some of the leading consulting engineers and road builders in the province, with participation by leading banks. Marshall Macklin Monaghan, the consulting engineers who had been actively involved in promoting design-build projects, was a member of this consortium. Among the other consulting engineering firms were McCormick Rankin and Delcan. The President of ORDC, Larry Tanenbaum, also led Warren Paving, one of the consortium's member construction firms.

ORDC had already approached the ministry about entering into an exclusive partnership to design, build and operate the highway. To obtain the best value for the taxpayers, Davies felt that there had to be a competition to deliver the project. This echoed the views of Pouliot and had the strong support of MTO staff. Practically though, competition this could have been difficult to achieve. ORDC appeared to have locked up most of the major players in Ontario, and no other Ontario-based consortium showed signs of emerging spontaneously.

Shortly before George Davies moved from Energy to MTO, a delegation from Agra Monenco, a large consulting engineering firm with a great deal of overseas experience, had met with him in a "show and tell" exercise. They had mentioned in passing that the firm's origins had been in designing highways in Saskatchewan. After Davies moved to MTO, he called Alex Taylor, the President of Agra Monenco, and asked him whether he would be interested in putting together a consortium to compete for Highway 407. A second Ontario-based consortium, led by Agra Monenco and later named Canadian Highways International Corporation (CHIC), was in fact formed, with similar capabilities to ORDC.

OBJECTIVES AND PRINCIPLES

A working group led by MTO, with support from the Ministry of Economic Development and Trade (MEDT), Treasury Board, Finance and Cabinet Office, continued development of an action plan. (This working group was formalized in March 1993 as the Highway 407 interministerial committee). The working group also engaged in discussions with both consortia. To that point, MTO had been proceeding without formal approvals by the government as a whole, though key personnel in the Premier's Office and the Cabinet Office were kept aware of developments. Jay Kaufman, the Deputy Secretary of Treasury Board and later Deputy Minister of Finance, was close to the Premier's advisers. Davies, who had known Kaufman previously when they had both been in the Manitoba public service, sought his counsel regularly to align the development of policy more closely with the thinking of Rae and his advisers.

By April 1993, MTO had prepared a preliminary action plan and was ready to proceed with its first formal step, namely a request for qualifications (RFQ) by consortia to carry out the Highway 407 project. The project's framework was now being defined with more precision. On a philosophical, or political basis, it was clear that governments could no longer fund major projects from the general tax base. The government now accepted user pay philosophies – a significant departure for the New Democratic Party. Recognizing that tolls were a novel approach to financing infrastructure in contemporary Ontario, the government, based on its consultations, believed that the public would accept tolls or fees that were dedicated to the facility that was being used.

Minister Pouliot then went to P&P to seek approvals and guidance in several areas. First, he sought confirmation of the government's commitment to the development of partnerships, a relatively new concept for the Ontario government. He also sought confirmation of the province's objectives before making further decisions on the project. Finally, he needed approval of the action plan. P&P was therefore asked to confirm the following objectives:

1. Reduction of cost and accelerated construction of the highway, as well as phasing construction to maximize revenue.
2. Project financing based on a business case and without provincial guarantees.
3. Development of strategic partnerships with the private sector.
4. Development of exportable expertise for Ontario-based companies in toll road construction, project management, project financing and electronic toll technology.
5. Establishment of benchmarks for cost reductions that might also be achieved on other provincial projects.
6. Retention of public policy flexibility, such as transit and high-occupancy vehicle lanes in the Highway 407 corridor and the ability to manage demand.

MTO undertook to adhere to a list of broad principles in delivering the project. It would obtain the best value for the Ontario public and would follow fair procurement practices. More significantly, it promised to seek out Ontario-first sourcing. This was a key principle, as job creation was the government's overall policy objective at that stage. It was also a potentially contentious one, as it could conflict with the first two principles – best value and fair procurement practices.

In the development of partnerships, MTO made a series of specific commitments. Competition would be to the final stage, as opposed to early selection of a single consortium and negotiations to an agreement with that party only. (This precluded selection of ORDC's proposal for an exclusive partnership.) Financial support would be provided for interim partnerships to allow them to develop. This was designed to keep the

ORDC consortium together. Members had been together for almost a year and some were talking of leaving now that they were faced with a competition, as opposed to the sole-source contract that they had anticipated. MTO wanted to pursue an Ontario-first concept, implicitly suggesting that Ontario-based consortia would receive any possible advantage over externally based ones. This was consistent with the desire to support development of exportable expertise by Ontario companies, but had to be handled delicately to avoid violating trade agreements.

P&P confirmed all the objectives and principles that MTO had proposed. It also established two clear principles when tolling roads. First, an alternate free route had to be available. Second, tolls would be removed when the highway had been paid for. Both principles left some room for debate. An alternate route was not necessarily a provincial freeway. In the case of Highway 407, this was in fact a freeway, Highway 401. In other possible cases, however, it could be interpreted to mean some combination of provincial and municipal roads. A definition of when the highway would be fully paid for was also lacking. In the opinion of some staff, this point would never be reached, as major maintenance and reconstruction expenses would be incurred periodically and would have to be paid for by tolls.

THE ACTION PLAN

MTO was aware of the risks involved in such a precedent setting undertaking. The action plan for the project was designed to minimize risk to the province and to allow for exit points, to enable the province to extricate itself, if it decided not to proceed at any stage.

MTO intended to begin the formal process with a request for qualifications (RFQ) as soon as P&P approved its plan. Even though the clear preference was for an Ontario-based consortium, it was decided to accept worldwide expressions of interest for qualification. It was anticipated that because of the short time frame, there would be limited external interest.

A value engineering phase would then follow, lasting from two to three months. In this stage, the qualified consortia would undertake a new conceptual approach to the project, including a review of standards and procedures. They would also produce sufficiently detailed designs to enable them to generate a guaranteed maximum price. MTO expected this phase would produce innovative designs and a new preliminary design that would ensure cost effectiveness. The consortia were both paid $1.5 million for their work in this phase. MTO also believed that paying the consortia for some work at this point would help to keep the more timorous ORDC members in the fold.

An RFP would then be issued, probably in mid-July 1993, and detailed proposals with a guaranteed maximum price accepted for evaluation from the qualified consortia. The target date for concluding the evaluation was November 1, 1993. It was anticipated that an agreement could be negotiated with the winning consortium before the end of 1993. In the meantime, construction of Highway 407 would continue to maintain employment. The action plan was approved by P&P. The schedule was ambitious, given the scale of the project. Although the actual process lagged by a few months, the sequence of actions went more or less as planned.

TOLLING TECHNOLOGY

To this point, the question of tolling technology had not been decided. There was consensus that electronic toll technology was the preferred option. Traditional tollbooths were impractical for an urban highway, with entrances and exits every few kilometres. A vast quantity of expensive urban property would have been required for toll plazas. In addition, traffic would back up on the feeder roads, creating congestion and causing safety problems.

MTO staff's preference was for an all-electronic tolling system, with drivers equipped with transponders that could be read by detectors as they entered and left the highway. Their tolling charge would be calculated and billed or deducted from a balance maintained in an account. In fact, the preference was for the transponder to be incorporated into the licence plate – the so-called electronic licence plate. This would give the flexibility to extend the system in the future to institute road pricing on other facilities as well. Staff envisaged a time when all major routes would be tolled and congestion pricing charges could be effortlessly levied in cities. It soon became apparent, however, that there was no political support for the electronic licence plate. The government did not feel it was necessary for Highway 407 and was unwilling to stir up controversy about the potential for tolling existing routes or expanding the user-pay concept. The limited application of electronic tolling to Highway 407 was accepted.

One of the issues with transponders was that they catered only to the frequent user of the highway. Occasional users were unlikely to make the investment in a transponder or deposit funds into an account that they would use only infrequently. The minister was particularly concerned that even occasional users should be able to use the highway. He often spoke of the imaginary Mrs. Brown from his northern Ontario riding of Lake Nipigon, who drove into Toronto with her cat, Fluffy, to see her children and wanted to use Highway 407.[2] He felt it was politically unacceptable that she be denied access to Highway 407 or fined because she did not have a transponder in her vehicle. He directed the ministry to develop options to allow for occasional users to drive on Highway 407, including the construction of tolling plazas at selected entrances and exits. A decision on this was deferred until June 1993.

REQUEST FOR QUALIFICATIONS

The way was now clear for the government to proceed with a request for qualifications from interested consortia. As expected, ORDC and CHIC submitted their qualifications for evaluation. To the government's surprise, a third consortium, led by the American firm, Peter Kiewit Sons, supported by the CIBC, also submitted their qualifications and a preliminary proposal. It was rejected for two reasons: its proposal to toll the express lanes of Highway 401 to pay for construction of Highway 407 was unacceptable to the government, and the firm's performance on a previous contract, the Burlington Interchange, had in MTO's view been substandard. On June 24, 1993, the premier announced that two consortia, ORDC and CHIC, had been selected to compete for Highway 407 project. The value engineering phase was now to commence.

VALUE ENGINEERING

On August 6, both consortia submitted their value engineering studies. These studies identified potential savings of $200 million. The biggest savings were achieved through the deferral of some interchanges, because traffic projections did not warrant them at that stage.[3] Additional savings were made by reduction in cost of certain structures. Finally, there was strict adherence to MTO's published standards for highways. This was to cause some controversy in the future because MTO had been exceeding these standards for some time. A number of factors were responsible, including over-engineering; i.e. increasing safety margins on individual projects beyond actual formal requirements.

Additionally, there was the effect of rounding after the conversion from imperial units to metric in the 1970s. For instance, the entrance lanes to highways had originally been specified as 500 yards. When the province had converted from the imperial to the metric system, this had simply been rounded up to 500 metres, whereas a direct conversion would have been 446 metres. Under the value engineering studies this was identified as a potential saving and entrance lanes were reduced in length to 446 metres. Most of the consortia's suggestions were incorporated in the RFP.

These studies proved another source of dissatisfaction within MTO. Staff felt they could have done just as effective a job on value engineering had they, too, been permitted to relax the constraints built into MTO's standards and procedures.

REQUEST FOR PROPOSALS

The final request for proposals was developed and issued on September 1, 1993. In it the government gave the consortia a considerable degree of latitude to propose innovative approaches. The government made it clear that it was looking for a partner who would finance, design, build, and operate the highway, including the tolling system, turning it over in good repair to the government after a given period of time.

Each consortium was allowed to submit only a single proposal. That proposal could contain within it more than one business arrangement. The proposals were to be comprehensive, containing details of the engineering and design, tolling, and financing. An all-electronic tolling system was to be in place by 1998, though a mixed manual - electronic system would be acceptable from 1996 to 1998.

Each of the components of the proposal was also to be disaggregated, so that the evaluating team could analyze each separately. A guaranteed maximum price was to be quoted for the design-build component. This was significant, as it gave the government the option to choose one or more of the components, without necessarily accepting the entire proposal.

Consistent with the government's attempt to minimize political involvement, the RFP explicitly prohibited lobbying, with stringent disqualification provisions. Finally, the deadline for submission of proposals was December 13, 1993.

EVALUATION

While the two consortia were preparing their proposals, the government was preparing to evaluate them. A proposal review committee was formed in October 1993. It was to report to MTO Deputy Minister Davies. The committee's mandate was to ensure the integrity of the evaluation and to synthesize the work of the evaluation teams. Specifically it would recommend and then institute the evaluation process, scrutinizing the proposals for the financial and technical aspects, as well as for compliance with the RFP.

Tony Salerno, who was now the Director of the Highway 407 project, and David Garner, a senior manager at MTO with extensive experience in highway design and construction, were co-chairs of this ten-member committee. Other members were drawn from the ministries represented on the inter-ministerial committee designing the project to that point. The committee was expected to use internal as well as external advisors to evaluate the different aspects of the proposals.

Confidentiality

Ensuring the confidentiality of the proposals, and of the evaluation process, was a key objective of the review committee. The government believed this to be necessary for several reasons. It wanted to eliminate attempts to interfere with or to influence the evaluation, and such attempts were held to be more likely if there were external knowledge of its progress. The government also needed to safeguard the proprietary information that would be in the proposals. It was acutely aware that the size of the contracts could have an impact on the stock market valuation of the companies involved and it wanted to ensure that there was no trading based on insider information about the evaluation in any of the companies involved in the consortia.

The proposals and evaluation documents therefore were to be kept in secure locations with access limited to those participating in the process. The proposals could be reviewed only in those secure locations. Removal and copying of documents was tightly controlled. Mylvaganam was given a tour of one of these locations soon after the proposals had been received, so that he could see the security measures that were in place. Great care was taken to ensure that he did not see the proposals or any documents relating to their evaluation.

Evaluation process

The proposal review committee began by developing an action plan. An evaluation process would be formulated, based on the RFP. The proposals would then be reviewed to ensure that all the issues raised in the RFP were addressed. They would also have to be internally consistent. The committee would report on the evaluation of the proposals and their comparative strengths and weaknesses relative to the evaluation criteria. The evaluation would form the basis of a submission to the Cabinet, which was expected to make the final decision.

There was a great deal of debate about how this decision-making by Cabinet would take place. It was ultimately decided that the staff would evaluate the proposals and determine the degree to which each criterion was met. Staff would also assess the relative strengths and weaknesses of the proposals. A blind selection process would then be structured and the information prepared by staff would be presented to the Cabinet to enable it to make its selection. This would be possible because neither the Cabinet nor their political staff were aware of the content of the proposals.

Six teams were formed to work on the different aspects of the evaluation. The engineering, construction, and operation team would assess the design, construction, delivery, maintenance, operation, and transfer elements of the proposals, including the maximum price to design and construct the facility. It would also carry out an appraisal of the value engineering submissions. The degree of technical innovation in the proposals, particularly as it pertained to tolling technology, was also to be considered, as were the demonstrated skill and ability of consortia members and their staff.

Another team would evaluate the overall viability of the business plan, including the financing plan. The degree of equity participation by consortia members would also be given consideration. In addition, this team would examine the proposed regulatory structure within the proposals, including mechanisms for regulating toll rates and expected rate of return, incentive rate, and protection against excessive rates of return. It would also consider the number of years before the highway was to be turned over to the government.

The toll rate team would look at the anticipated aggregate toll rate and other sources of revenue, as well as the degree to which toll revenues were expected to support the project. The risk assessment team would assess all elements of risk, especially financial and operational.

Another team was responsible for evaluating the fiscal impact on the province. This would include the degree to which the government's financial exposure was minimized; an important factor for the government, which had seen previous governments excessively exposed in various deals with the private sector. A final team would evaluate the industrial benefits that would accrue to the province.

Attempting to minimize controversy

The government was aware that the size and unprecedented nature of the project were bound to make it controversial. It anticipated that the unsuccessful consortium would be unhappy at having lost out on such a lucrative contract. Furthermore, the political opposition, though it supported the project, would be looking for areas in which it could criticize the government's handling of it. The Cabinet tried to minimize this risk by distancing itself from the evaluation of the proposals, so that it could not be credibly accused of political interference.

The Highway 407 inter-ministerial committee also realized that because of the open-ended nature of the RFP, the proposals would be sufficiently dissimilar for the evaluation to include many subjective elements. After some internal discussion, the committee decided that the weighting assigned to the different criteria for evaluation listed in the RFP would not be made public. There were several reasons for this decision. Because the RFP had asked for disaggregation of the project's components – design, tolling, construction, and finance – the evaluation team was able to consider different combinations. This made a simple weighting system complex and cumbersome. Also, they recognized that they were learning as they went along and feared that being locked into a set of weights at this stage could impair the effectiveness of the evaluation. There was a developing consensus that the weighting system would evolve alongside evaluation of the bid components. A further reason for not divulging the weights was to make it impossible for the losing consortium to second-guess the evaluation itself. As we will see, this approach brought mixed consequences.

Lobbying

Though the RFP explicitly prohibited lobbying, both consortia retained lobbyists. ORDC had retained SAMCI (formerly Susan A. Murray Consulting Inc.). CHIC employed Corporation House. (Interestingly, the principals of both firms had strong links to the Ontario Conservatives.) Given the restrictions on lobbying, and the highly confidential nature of the evaluation process, once the RFP was underway there was very little the lobbyists could influence, or even ascertain. The main role of these consultants seemed to be to assure their clients that the process was unfolding as it should and that the other party did not have it "locked up." Mylvaganam would periodically receive phone calls from the two consultants wanting to know whether everything was "on track." Other members of the government would receive queries about the status of the project as an aside in unrelated interactions. That was the limit of contact with the political side of the government. Indeed, Minister Pouliot took Premier Rae's principle of distance to the point of deliberately avoiding meetings with principals of either consortium while the process was underway. The impact of the Premier's injunction was evident. Lobbying by the consortia had no impact on the process or the evaluation. Despite these precautions, controversy did develop, as we will see.

Tolling partners

Both consortia were essentially composed of construction, engineering, and financial partners. The tolling partners were later additions to the groups, joining them as late as August 1993. This was partly because the technology could not simply be purchased off the shelf. All-electronic tolling systems had been used elsewhere, but all users were expected to have some type of transponder or detection device. The requirement that occasional users be accommodated meant that a more complex, in fact, a unique system had to be developed. No single company had as yet developed the tolling system necessary for such a venture. To ensure that this critical component of the project was delivered, Davies and his senior staff approached different companies to form a consortium. Bell Canada appeared to be an obvious choice for the billing system. The parallels between billing for usage of varying distances of the highway and for long-distance phone usage seemed self-evident. Some form of licence plate recognition would be needed to handle users who did not have transponders. Hughes Aircraft had developed high-resolution imaging for targeting cruise missiles that had been deployed during the Gulf War. This was ideal for imaging licence plates, and Davies approached Hughes as well. Finally, Bell Sygma, the systems management arm of Bell Canada, was brought in to integrate the different components.

This tolling group, comprising Bell Canada, Bell Sygma, and Hughes Aircraft joined the ORDC consortium. Mark IV Industries would supply transponders to this group. Sirit Technologies, a Canadian company with some experience with electronic tolling systems, entered the competition by allying itself with the CHIC consortium. The RFP had specifically denied exclusivity between the civil consortia and the providers of tolling technology. This gave the government the option of choosing the civil consortium from one team and the tolling partner from another – a flexibility it would, in fact, exploit.

The labour agreement

Both consortia were approached by a group of construction unions, the Labourers International Union of North America (LIUNA) local 183, Brotherhood of Teamsters local 230, and International Union of Operating Engineers local 793, which offered to sign a no strike - no lockout agreement for the duration of the project. CHIC negotiated such an agreement and signed it on January 7, 1994. ORDC, however, felt the agreement CHIC had entered into was too restrictive. It therefore did not complete the negotiations that had been in process for some time. ORDC claimed that it was uncomfortable with signing an exclusive agreement with three unions that could shut out others, such as the Carpenters, Electricians and Ironworkers, as well as keep other subcontractors off the project. It also claimed subsequently that David Guscott, Assistant Deputy Minister for Policy and Planning in MTO, had stated that it should not sign such an agreement if it was uncomfortable with it.

Some within the labour movement have a different view. They believe that ORDC did not want to sign such an exclusive agreement because some of its partners and affiliated companies were not unionized – a potential source of labour problems in the future.

Ironically, given the government's elaborate precautions, this seemingly insignificant issue gave rise to the greatest controversy surrounding the highway. We discuss the controversy itself in Chapter 5.

The proposals

The proposals were received on December 13, 1993 and evaluation commenced as planned. Both consortia had submitted comprehensive proposals that met the requirements of the RFP. Each would deliver the facility faster and at a lower cost than envisaged. Neither was seeking any provincial cash contributions. In view of the size of the project and uncertainty about user acceptance, both consortia sought government guarantees for financing. These guarantees would be drawn upon in the event of a shortfall in anticipated tolling revenues.

There were significant differences between the proposals. CHIC had proposed a concrete highway; ORDC a more traditional asphalt pavement. While CHIC would build a 6-lane highway at the outset, ORDC would initially build a 4-lane highway, adding lanes after traffic volumes grew sufficiently. The approaches to tolling also differed. The Bell Canada/Bell Sygma/Hughes tolling arm of ORDC proposed a fully electronic tolling system. CHIC's affiliate, Sirit, proposed a mixed electronic and manual system.

DIRECTION FROM P&P

On January 17, 1994, P&P was presented with a progress report on the evaluation. The proposal review committee wanted its direction on some policy questions, as well as approval of the decision-making approach that it was proposing. Perhaps most significantly, the choice of the successful consortium was to be made by a committee of four deputy ministers and not by the Cabinet as previously envisaged. Strictly speaking, the committee would make a recommendation to the board of the recently proclaimed Ontario Transportation Capital Corporation (OTCC), which would formalize the decision. (OTCC was a Crown corporation responsible for developing the highway. It is described more fully in Chapter 6.) This was to be done because OTCC now had responsibility for the project. Since the OTCC did not have any external directors at that point, this was merely a formality. All the members of the OTCC board were public servants who had been significantly involved in the recommendation. Cabinet's role would be limited to making decisions about major policy and fiscal issues.

A committee of deputy ministers had previously been used when the government had selected a private sector partner for the construction and operation of a government-owned casino. The present committee comprised George Davies (Transportation), Jay Kaufman (Finance), Peter Barnes (MEDT) and Judith Wolfson (Consumer and Corporate Affairs). The first three were obvious choices. They, or their staff, had been an integral part of the project design to that point. Wolfson was included because her ministry had been responsible for two previous partnerships with the private sector - the casino project and Teranet, the electronic land registry. It was felt that the experience she had gained in those exercises would be useful. The committee would use input from the proposal review committee to make its decision.

This approach was adopted because the government felt that Cabinet would not add any value to the actual selection of one of the consortia. Cabinet's proper role was to make policy decisions, entrusting public servants to make the specific decisions necessary to implement those policies. Once again, the (unstated) desire to insulate the government from the inevitable allegations of political influence was clearly in operation.

At this time, P&P also confirmed the province's objectives: maximization of project-based financing, without recourse to the province; public toll rate setting and review; and the flexibility to introduce high-occupancy vehicle lanes and rapid transit within the corridor at a future date. It also wanted an option for public financing, with private sector design, build, operate, and transfer to be developed.

P&P was asked to provide guidance on some of the key questions facing the evaluation teams. These included the size of the premium in cost and risk that the province would be prepared to pay for the private sector to handle all aspects of the project (design, build, finance, and operate) and the ideal ratio of equity between the province and a successful consortium. Other issues related to operation of the highway and return to investors: whether toll rates should be tied to inflation and the acceptable rate of return for the private sector. Finally, it was asked to consider the implications for the province of the size and condition of guarantees in the event of shortfalls in toll revenues.

The requests for financial guarantees were troubling for the government. Previous governments had a record of assuming the debt for projects that private interests had undertaken, such as the Skydome, at significant cost to the province. The Rae government was cynical about guarantees. Guarantees, it felt, did little more than insulate the private sector from risk, while allowing it to reap the rewards from a project.

There was discussion on how the government should respond to the requests for guarantees. One option was to go back to the consortia and ask them to revise their proposals by removing this request. Adjustments to the financing portion of the proposals would inevitably lead to delays, and, as noted earlier, the government was anxious to accelerate the project. The cost of the proposals would also rise because, without guarantees, the costs of financing the project would be higher.

The other option was for the government to take over the financing of the project and allow the private sector to design, build, and operate the highway. This would be an abandonment of many aspects of the partnership as originally envisaged and all financial risk would now be vested with the government. For the government, the risk would be the same in either case. It would, however, be able to borrow to finance the highway more cheaply than could the private sector, even with government guarantees. The benefits of design-build elaborated earlier would still be attainable. Both these options were possible because the RFP had asked for the different components of the proposal to be disaggregated and also for a guaranteed maximum price for the design-build component of the project.

P&P decided that because of the request for provincial financial guarantees, the originally envisaged approach of acceptance of a single proposal for the private sector to design, build, own, finance, operate, and ultimately transfer the highway was no longer feasible. It asked for two options to be developed for further consideration. Under a public financing option, the OTCC would finance the highway, which would be developed under a design-build-operate agreement. Under a negotiated private financing option, the best design, construction, operations and financing terms from both proposals would be selected to make up a single composite project. In the meantime, to minimize delays, MTO was directed to continue tendering approximately $150 million of construction contracts on Highway 407 for the upcoming 1994 construction season. The successful consortium would take over responsibility for these contracts once it had been selected.

THE FUNDRAISING DINNER

On January 20, 1994, barely a month after the proposals had been submitted, the three unions which had signed the no strike-no lockout agreement with CHIC held a fundraising dinner for the NDP at the Labourers' International Union of North America Local 183's banquet hall in Downsview. The function, billed as "An evening of appreciation for the Premier," was the biggest fundraising event in the history of the Ontario NDP and raised over $100,000. Most of the key figures in the government were there, including the Premier and almost all the cabinet. (Ironically, Pouliot, the minister overseeing Highway 407 project, as well as many of the other infrastructure projects of the government, was not present, since he had returned to his riding of Lake Nipigon in Northwest Ontario for the weekend.)

Also in attendance were all the major players in ORDC and CHIC, most of whom had never been to any kind of NDP function in their lives, though they were hardly strangers at events associated with the Conservatives or Liberals. They viewed attendance as a show of goodwill towards a government that was about to make a decision that could give them sizeable economic benefits.

Speeches at the dinner by politicians and union leaders lauded the government's commitment to funding infrastructure. The acceleration of Highway 407, the proposal to build four subway lines in Toronto, and the new Metro Toronto convention centre, all major generators of employment for the construction industry, were highlighted.

After the contract was awarded, this event would be interpreted in the media as evidence of union influence on the decision, as will be discussed in Chapter 5.

FINAL STAGES OF THE EVALUATION

The evaluation teams continued their work under the direction of the Proposal Review Committee, which synthesized and consolidated their analyses for the deputies' committee. The deputies' committee verified the analyses and assigned weights for the different aspects of the selection criteria. It was given separate presentations by each of the consortia and also interviewed them. Based on all these, the deputies committee was almost ready to make its recommendation. Before doing so, it sought ratification from P&P of some critical policy recommendations.

P&P met on March 28, 1994 to consider the policy recommendations made by the deputies' committee. It was still unaware of the specific content of the individual proposals, though it was made aware of elements of each, without identification of the proponent.

The government had chosen the public financing option, with the private sector to design, build, and operate the highway. It did so because of its concern about the risk posed by the private sector's request for a provincial guarantee, and this was the approach strongly supported by the bureaucracy. The arguments presented by staff were as follows. Even if the successful consortium's financing were fully guaranteed by the government, its financing costs would be approximately 0.25% higher than if the borrowing were directly by a Crown corporation such as the OTCC. This would add an estimated $30 million in net present value to the cost. The consortium could potentially raise approximately $200 million on a non-recourse basis (that is, guaranteed by the project itself rather than any of their other assets). However, financing costs would exceed potential crown financing costs by 0.3 to 0.7%, adding an estimated $35 to $100 million to the cost of the project. Private sector equity finance would also require a return on the order of 12%, which would further increase project costs. Overall, therefore, the cost of the project would be increased and these increased costs, the government feared, would make it more likely that the province would have to provide the funding it guaranteed. The question arose whether the OTCC, if it financed the highway, would have to call on the government to subsidize it. Sensitivity analyses were performed, varying parameters such as traffic volumes, interest rates and inflation, and taking into account factors such as possible construction delays, environmental remediation, an inability or unwillingness to raise tolls to sufficient levels to meet revenue requirements and changes to the project scope. The likely range of scenarios showed that the risk of having to subsidize was negligible. Accordingly, the Minister of Finance and the OTCC were authorized to provide appropriate debt financing for the project. In other words, P&P ratified the new vision of the project. The original concept had been of a highway entirely financed, designed, built, and operated by the private sector, where it took all the financial risk. This had been replaced by a strategic partnership, where the private sector designed, built, and operated the highway, and the government used its advantages to finance it. Funding would be project-based and guaranteed by the revenue stream from the project – a significant departure from previous practice of the Ontario government or its agencies.

It is worth noting here that even when the project was being designed, several key participants believed that the government would ultimately finance it. They based the belief on the reasoning that, as shown above, the government could borrow at lower cost than the private sector. Unless a company was willing to self-finance to win the contract at a lower cost, costs would always be lower with government financing. It was also their opinion that such self-financing was unlikely with Canadian companies, which, they felt, tended to be risk averse.

The government decided that an all-electronic tolling system would be used. As described earlier, preference for this option over one that also included manual toll collection had been growing as the project was being developed. The choice was also seen as facilitating development of exportable expertise, as there was growing international demand for proven all-electronic toll systems. With this system, vehicles would be equipped with electronic transponders that would be detected when they entered and left the highway. All commercial vehicles, including those from out of province, would be required to enroll in the electronic toll program and equip their vehicles with transponders. Video plate capture, supplemented by photo billing, would be used to accommodate occasional users, who did not have transponders. Their licence plates would be digitally imaged when they entered and left the highway. The cost of their trip would be calculated, based on the distance traveled and they would receive invoices, including a small surcharge. Sanctions could be employed against Ontario-registered vehicles that did not pay these invoices. Out-of-province, non-commercial vehicles could simply ignore them, however, as there was no method of penalizing non-payment. The OTCC was directed to pursue inter-jurisdictional enforcement agreements and the government prepared to receive complaints that it was giving non-Ontarians a free ride.

The government directed the OTCC to develop and implement a mechanism to set toll rates. It also decided that toll rates would be subject to approval by the cabinet. This decision stemmed from the realization that, despite OTCC's formal arms-length relationship with the government, as a Crown corporation it would be portrayed as part of the government. The government was not prepared entirely to relinquish control over decisions that could have a public and therefore a political impact.

Everything was now ready for the selection of the private sector partner by the Deputies' Committee and the OTCC. The announcement was scheduled for Friday, April 8, 1994.

CHAPTER 5

CHOICE AND CRITICISM

THE ANNOUNCEMENT

The announcement of the contract award was to be made on April 8, 1994. In preparation, MTO's communications department worked closely with Murray Weppler, a consultant with extensive experience with NDP governments across Canada, to develop a communications plan. Key themes included the "good news" of job creation and the preservation of the transit and other policy options in the corridor, as well as a more critical contrasting of this process with the very controversial redevelopment of the terminals at Pearson Airport.

The Toronto Stock Exchange had been notified that an announcement on the Highway 407 contracts was to be made on April 8, so that it could monitor the shares of member firms of the two consortia for any unusual trading activity. Armbro Enterprises, the parent of one of the contractors belonging to the CHIC consortium, had been in some financial difficulty and its share price had fallen to little over a dollar. There was some excitement on April 7, when its shares almost doubled in value. This was later attributed merely to speculation in a depressed stock with the perceived potential to increase in value very quickly.

On the evening of April 7, the Deputies' Committee met and made its recommendation. This was quickly ratified by the board of the OTCC, whose membership overlapped that of the committee. The political arm of government had remained insulated from the actual selection and was not yet aware of the decision.

On the morning of April 8, at approximately 7:30 a.m., Davies telephoned the Premier to inform him that CHIC had been selected as the successful consortium for the civil works. At the same time, Assistant Deputy Minister for Policy and Planning David Guscott briefed Chandran Mylvaganam, the minister's chief of staff, in the minister's boardroom in the Ferguson Building at Queen's Park. Mylvaganam telephoned the minister to inform him of the decision.

The two consortia were to assemble in conference rooms in separate hotels in close proximity to Queen's Park. The deputies and senior MTO staff would then visit each hotel in turn to brief each consortium on the decision. CHIC was briefed first, at 8:15 a.m. at the Westbury Hotel. Apparently, Davies' initial remarks dwelt on the deficiencies in CHIC's proposal to such an extent that the consortium believed it had not been selected. ORDC had their briefing at 8:45 a.m. at the Sutton Place Hotel. Disappointed that it had not been chosen, members had still come prepared for that eventuality. Immediately after hearing the news, the chairman, Larry Tanenbaum, handed Davies a letter withdrawing ORDC's proposal. ORDC later stated it wished to avoid an auction-like situation, if negotiations between the OTCC and CHIC broke down.

The consortia were also informed that the government had decided to use an all-electronic tolling system. It would work with CHIC to reach an agreement with the Bell Canada/Bell Sygma/Hughes tolling group which had been affiliated with the unsuccessful ORDC consortium. This group had offered an all-electronic system, while SIRIT, which had been affiliated with CHIC, had proposed a mixed electronic – manual system. In the event that no agreement was reached with the Bell group, the government could still call upon SIRIT. SIRIT seemed to believe this meant they had an equal chance to supply the toll system. As negotiations with the Bell group dragged on for several months, they began to express loud concerns that the OTCC had not yet begun to negotiate with them.

ORDC'S REACTION

ORDC's disappointment at its failure was proportionate to its earlier confidence and would prove to have significant political repercussions. The debriefing for members of the consortium who had not attended their presentation to the Deputies' Committee had been decidedly upbeat. ORDC had constituted itself as a consortium long before CHIC and had been discussing the possibility of sole sourcing the project with MTO as early as 1992. It could not believe that CHIC, which had been formed only just prior to the commencement of the competition, could have submitted a superior proposal. It was also disappointed that the government had chosen to separate the components of the proposal and to finance the highway itself. ORDC felt that had the proposals been accepted in their entirety, theirs would have been chosen. It also claimed that had it known that the financing was to be separated, it would have submitted a different type of proposal. A leading member of the ORDC consortium later told Mylvaganam that it had expected the government to come back to negotiate the issue of provincial guarantees. It had certainly never expected the government to take over financing of the project in its entirety.

Some members of ORDC suspected that their refusal – and CHIC's willingness – to sign an agreement with the construction unions had prejudiced the NDP government's evaluation of their bid. This suspicion, too, would return to trouble the government.

INITIAL POLITICAL REACTION

ORDC was not alone in being surprised by the committee's decision. Minister Pouliot, too, was unprepared for the result. Like most others who had been involved in the process from the outset and had met members of the ORDC consortium, he tended to view it as the more experienced consortium, better able to handle the project. CHIC had appeared later on the scene, much closer to the point at which the cautions about contact with the consortia had been issued by the Premier. It had not had the same level of contact with the minister or other members of the government. As a result, its capabilities were not as well known.

The government was, nonetheless, very satisfied with the project's progress to that point. The highway would be delivered by 1997, instead of the originally estimated 2020. It would cost approximately 20 % less than the original estimates. True, the highway would not be financed by the private sector. Financing would be project based, however, at no direct cost to the Treasury, so even here the government felt a measure of satisfaction.

This should not suggest complacency. Certainly the government anticipated that ORDC would be unhappy. It also expected that the opposition parties in the legislature would try to find fault with the process. Still, it felt that by insulating the political arm of government from the evaluation and decision making processes, it had successfully armed itself against the type of controversy that had plagued the federal Conservatives during the Pearson airport fiasco. Though the proposals themselves and the evaluations were to remain confidential, the process had been overseen by Price Waterhouse, who would certify that it been entirely above board.

The questions and answers prepared for government spokespeople reflected this confidence. They focused on the process that had been followed, the next steps, and the approach to financing, which was thought likely to be the most contentious issue.

The initial stories in the media were positive and were consistent with the message the government had striven for. They highlighted the acceleration of the highway and job creation during construction. The financing by the government was portrayed as further lowering the cost of the highway, thereby reducing toll rates.

CONTROVERSY

Despite the government's satisfaction with both the contracting process and its outcome, it did not take long for controversy to develop. The Conservatives and Liberals in the legislature called for the release of the proposals and evaluation documents to satisfy themselves that the correct decision had been made. The government refused on two publicly stated grounds. First, the final contracts still had to be negotiated with CHIC. Secondly, and more fundamentally, it felt that the confidentiality of the proposals, which had in fact been requested by both consortia, had to be maintained, to preserve the competitive positions of both when pursuing future projects. The government also felt that the public and the legislature should be satisfied by the certification of Price Waterhouse that the competition had been fairly conducted. There was also an underlying concern that because the evaluations were so complex and subjective – two very different proposals were being compared – it would be quite easy to make a case that the process was flawed. This refusal by the government only served to stoke the controversy. The media and the opposition began using adjectives such as "secretive" to characterize the process. The implication, of course, was that the government had something to hide.

On April 18 a story ran in *The Hamilton Spectator* and other newspapers in the Southam chain (Casella 1993). The headline read "Highway deal goes to NDP fundraisers" and the story began, "The three construction unions responsible for the biggest fundraiser in Ontario NDP history have won an exclusive deal to build the new $1 billion highway....". While the reporter was careful not to make any specific allegations of wrongdoing by the government, the story was laced with insinuations that the contract had been awarded to CHIC as an indirect way of rewarding the unions for their support of the NDP. The labour agreement and the fundraising dinner of January 20 (see Chapter 4) were cited as evidence. Gerry Phillips, the Liberals' finance critic, was quoted decrying the confidentiality surrounding the contract award, because it did not allow people to know whether the best possible price had been obtained for the highway. The Conservatives' Chris Stockwell was less judicious in his criticism. He scoffed at the notion that the cabinet had distanced itself from the decision making process by delegating it to a committee of deputy ministers. Since the deputies had to answer to their ministers in any case, he asserted such delegation was meaningless. According to him, the process "smelled."

The argument that the labour agreement had played a part in the award was given some credibility by Bill Pearson of CHIC, who was quoted in the article as saying that the assurance of labour peace had been attractive to the government. This was further bolstered by a remark reportedly made by Tony Salerno, the director of the 407 project, to the effect that it was important to the government that the winning consortium be able to guarantee labour peace for the life of the contract. Salerno later maintained that his statement had been inaccurately reported and not placed in context. He had been speaking in general terms, stating the obvious: that no government would want labour unrest on a major project. He emphatically denied that the labour agreement had played any part in the evaluation. The damage, however, had been done.

More questions were asked in the legislature (Hansard 1994a, 1994b, 1994c). The Liberals persisted in demanding that the government release the proposals and evaluation. They also questioned the decision to finance the highway publicly, characterizing this as a failure on the government's part. The Conservatives adopted a more strident tone. They had consistently attacked the NDP government for being close to organized labour. The allegation that the Highway 407 contract had been awarded to CHIC as a reward to labour unions fitted neatly into this approach. Their transportation critic, David Turnbull, liberally sprinkled his questions to the minister with references to "your union buddies." Turnbull's questioning was particularly aggressive. Members of the ORDC consortium were supplying him with questions about the technical aspects of the evaluation. For example, one day he asked Minister Pouliot about the life-cycle costs of concrete versus asphalt highways, questioning whether CHIC's concrete highway was in fact the low cost alternative.

And there was more controversy. Armbro Enterprises Inc., the parent company of Armbro Holdings, a member of CHIC, had filed for bankruptcy some months earlier and was in the process of being reorganized. Turnbull attacked the government for awarding the contract to a consortium with a partner that might not be in a position to carry out the contract. He accused the government of incompetence and demanded that the Highway 407 contract be re-tendered.

The minister's responses were generally the same, whatever the question. First, Pouliot would express his delight, in the most effusive language, that the highway was to be built faster, cheaper, and at no cost to the taxpayers. Then, he would reaffirm his faith in the integrity of the process, citing the certification of the process by Price Waterhouse and the fact that the decision had been made by four deputy ministers. He would often contrast this with the Pearson airport process, to take a jab at the Conservatives. Occasionally, he would praise the competence of the technical experts who had carried out the evaluation. Turnbull, who never received a direct answer to any of his questions, would be near apoplexy by the time he asked a supplementary question, which would receive similar treatment. When Pouliot had finished his now-familiar response, Turnbull would be shouting at him and would often have to be asked by the Speaker to restrain himself (Hansard 1994c).

Pouliot would confess to his staff that he was sometimes frustrated at being unable to answer more fully. He was satisfied that the correct decision had been made, because he had confidence in the civil servants who had made it. By design, he was unaware of the facts needed to reply fully to the questions he was being asked, because of the decision to insulate ministers from the decision making process. The confidentiality of the proposals also had to be considered when responding to questions. He was aware that his non-responsiveness was being characterized as evidence that the government was hiding something, but felt that his hands were tied – an unforeseen and certainly unintended consequence of the government's principle of strict separation.

The unrelenting questions were of concern to CHIC as well. It was unhappy that controversy was being attached to its hard-earned success and feared this could reflect on the member companies of the consortium. CHIC wanted the government to be more aggressive in its defense of the process and the selection of CHIC. The government in its turn suggested that CHIC should ask the opposition, with which its principals had good connections, to tone down the attacks. CHIC met with little success. Finally, in the hope of quieting the critics, CHIC agreed to the release of its proposal, provided that ORDC waived confidentiality of its proposal as well. ORDC did not agree, and the suggestion came to nothing.

After a few weeks, the furor died down, but the impression had been created that something untoward had taken place. Questions in the legislature continued to be raised from time to time, mostly calling for release of documents.

The controversy was likely exacerbated by the fact that ORDC had not received an in-depth post award briefing. MTO's inclination was to conduct such a briefing. It felt that the consortium, which had invested so much time and money in its bid, deserved to know why it had not been selected, and believed it would accept the outcome once it knew the reasons. ORDC was threatening to sue the government, however, and the legal advice was that such a briefing would not be prudent while the threat of a lawsuit existed.

A summary of the Development, Design, and Build Agreement, including the guaranteed maximum price of $929.8 million, was released in June 1994 when MTO appeared before the legislature's Standing Committee on Estimates. The government stood firm in its position that no further information about the content of the proposals could be released.

Contracts of this magnitude are of immense importance to the bidders. When, as is almost always the case, there are few bidders and when, as in this instance, the perceived front-runner did not receive the contract, it is likely that the losing bidder will think it has been treated unfairly. Contracts of this magnitude are also of great significance to the media and the opposition, and both will be looking for evidence of irregularities in the process. In our concluding chapter we consider what can be done to ensure that the contracting process be both fair, ex ante, and perceived to be fair, ex post.

CONTRACT NEGOTIATIONS

Negotiations with CHIC concluded on May 11, 1994. A contract to develop, design and build Highway 407 for a distance of 69 kilometres from Highway 48 (Markham Road) in the east to Highway 403 in the west was finalized with CHIC and its constituent companies (see map). This negotiation was relatively straightforward, as it was based on CHIC's proposal. Negotiations with the tolling consortium of Bell Canada, Bell Sygma, and Hughes would be the next step and were likely to be more complex, as the two consortia were coming together for the first time.

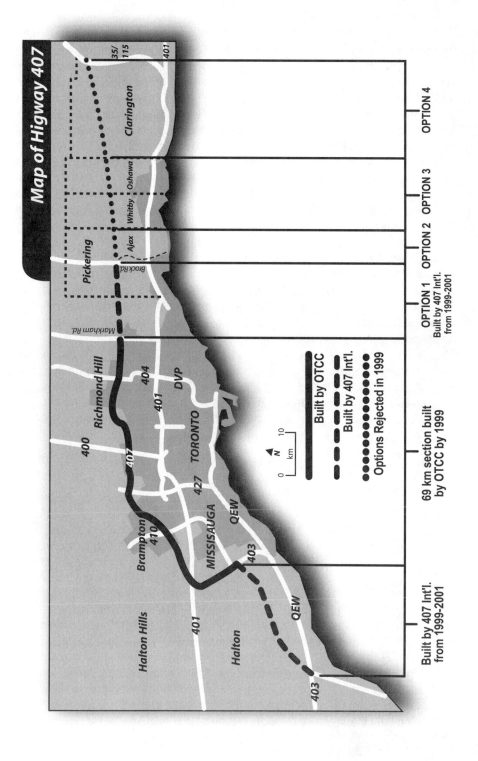

Map of Higway 407

49

It was George Davies who had brought the tolling consortium together. Its constituent companies had not worked together before, however, and were now being asked to negotiate a three-way agreement with the OTCC and yet another new consortium, CHIC. The negotiations consequently took much longer than the government had anticipated. They were finally concluded and an agreement signed on September 15, 1995. The delay did not have an impact on the civil works, but it did affect the start of work on the tolling system. (The development of the tolling system is discussed in Chapter 7.)

A NEW MINISTER

In October 1994, the Minister of Northern Development resigned from the cabinet. In the minor cabinet shuffle that ensued, Pouliot was appointed to that portfolio, and Mike Farnan, the associate minister of Education, replaced him at Transportation. At the request of the Premier's office, most of Pouliot's senior political staff remained at Transportation with Farnan, to maintain continuity.

Farnan was soon brought up to speed on the Highway 407 file and maintained the same position as Pouliot with respect to confidentiality of the proposals and the evaluation. He was asked a few questions in the legislature on the subject, but the issue appeared to have lost its urgency.

HIGHWAY 407 EAST (AND WEST)

After a briefing by senior MTO staff regarding the evaluation of their proposal, ORDC had come to terms with the selection of CHIC to build Highway 407. It felt strongly, however, that while the consortium had the capability of handling similar projects, it needed a project of comparable importance if it was to remain together. In the summer of 1994, ORDC approached senior staff at MTO and began discussing the possibility of building the eastern extension of 407, from Highway 48 (Markham Road) to Highway 35/115 (see map) under an exclusive agreement. This stage was more complex than the original 407 project because the environmental assessment work had not yet been carried out.

Receiving what they felt were encouraging signals, on July 25, 1994, ORDC submitted an unsolicited proposal to accelerate delivery of Highway 407 East. The proposal was a fully integrated work plan and included, among other features, overall management of the process, a fast track environmental assessment process, value engineering and development engineering in parallel, overall management, development of a comprehensive financial plan, construction management services, and provision of an optional guaranteed maximum price. Under this proposal, Highway 407 East would be completed by the year 2000, at least 10 years ahead of the best-case scenario at that point.

ORDC then engaged in further discussions with MTO staff and addressed a number of issues in the proposal. It reviewed the proposal with the minister's staff, who had been unaware of the extent of the discussions to that time. It also met with municipal and provincial political leaders to gain their political support.

In the meantime, MTO had been formulating a two-stage plan to accelerate Highway 407 East. On December 12, 1994, it went to P&P for approval to proceed with the first significant steps. The first stage, for which approval was now sought, called for consolidation of environmental assessment approval and preliminary design and value engineering as a single contract that would be tendered by a competitive process. The second stage, construction of the highway, would be undertaken only if it were determined that it would be self-financing. This first stage combined the front-end elements of the ORDC proposal, but, by severing the detailed engineering and construction, and most importantly by going out for tender, it essentially superseded it. At the same meeting, MTO also requested permission to seek proposals for the Western extension of Highway 407, to link up with the Queen Elizabeth Way (see map). P&P directed MTO to return with the results of a stakeholder consultation before approval was given.

ORDC now began hearing from MTO staff that the government was considering accelerating Highway 407 East, but that their proposal was unlikely to be accepted. It wrote to the Premier on February 3, 1995 expressing concern at this turn of events and urging again that the government adopt its proposal. At the request of the Premier's Office, a meeting was arranged between Farnan and ORDC Chairman Larry Tanenbaum at very short notice. Prior to the meeting, Mylvaganam was told by the Premier's office that they would support sole sourcing of the first phase to ORDC, if Farnan wished to do so.

At the meeting Tanenbaum, and Dale Patterson, Executive Vice President at Morrison Hershfield, one of the members of the ORDC consortium, made their case to Farnan, who was accompanied by his senior political staff. Tanenbaum and Patterson informed Farnan that they had spoken to the Liberal and Conservative leaders and obtained their assurances that they would not object if ORDC's unsolicited proposal was accepted. The possibility of limiting the contract to the first phase was also discussed. Farnan listened to their arguments and deferred his decision. Following the meeting, he met with his staff to discuss the issue.

Farnan was a cautious minister. He had been appointed to Rae's first cabinet in 1990, but had been dropped in less than a year following a controversy that dragged on for several months. An over-zealous staffer in Farnan's constituency office had written on behalf of constituents to a justice of the peace about parking tickets that had been erroneously issued, sparking allegations about political interference with the judiciary. The controversy had cost Farnan his seat in the cabinet, unfairly as he felt. He had rehabilitated himself by working hard, first as a backbencher and then as Associate Minister of Education. He had already experienced the feeding frenzy that any real or perceived ministerial transgression set off in the opposition and in the media. He was determined not to let it happen again.

It was evident at the outset that he did not support sole sourcing the contract to ORDC. An election was likely to be called within a few months and he felt that the opposition could not be trusted to forgo criticism at this politically heated time, despite their apparent assurances to ORDC. Indeed, he thought they could be trying to set him up. He also did not place any faith in the Premier's Office's concurrence with a sole sourced contract, as he did not feel that they would necessarily stand by him if he came under criticism. MTO staff did not recommend sole sourcing to ORDC either. The first phase was worth several million dollars. The entire project would cost well over a $100 million. In their opinion, a competitive tendering process was essential to secure the best value for the province.

Farnan wrote to ORDC on February 15 that the government intended to proceed with a two-stage competitive process, because the "Ontario public must be satisfied that the government is receiving the best possible deal." On February 20, P&P approved the plan.

On March 31, Premier Rae announced in Whitby that the province would seek private sector partners to accelerate planning and design of the 62-kilometre eastern section of Highway 407, from Highway 48 (Markham Rd.) to Highway 35/115. It would soon request qualifications and proposals from groups of firms capable of doing environmental assessments, traffic forecasts and preliminary design, as well as exploring options for private sector financing. Farnan made a parallel announcement in Oakville. The government intended to complete the 22-kilometre western section of Highway 407, from the Mississauga – Oakville border, the western end of the portion of Highway 407 under construction, to the Queen Elizabeth Way in Burlington (see map).

In April the government sought requests for qualifications for both projects. At the end of the month a provincial election was called and work on these projects stalled while the campaign was underway.

THE NEW GOVERNMENT

The Conservatives under Mike Harris defeated the Rae government in the election that took place in June 1995. Within a few weeks of taking office, the new government stopped work on the two RFQs that had been issued. While the NDP government's plans to complete Highway 407 in both the east and the west came to naught, the Conservatives would continue to deal with this issue in subsequent years.

The responsible ministers in the new government were briefed on the Highway 407 selection processes and the contract. The recollection of staff who participated in those briefings is that most of the ministers felt that there were no substantive issues regarding either to be addressed. In their view, the criticisms had merely been political gamesmanship. The exception was the new Chair of Management Board, David Johnson, who came into office apparently believing the various charges his party had made while in opposition. After the briefings, however, he seemed satisfied that everything had been above board. (David Turnbull, the most vociferous critic, was not appointed to Harris' initial cabinet.) The new government decided that the issues they had apparently found so disturbing while in opposition, and the legislative inquiry they had called for during the election campaign, were no longer worth pursuing. The contracts that had been issued on Highway 407 proceeded without any changes.

Nothing further happened on Highway 407 East for over a year. In late 1996, MTO initiated an environmental assessment for the much more limited section of Highway 407 East from Highway 48 to Brock Road in Pickering (see map). This was completed and received approval from the Minister of the Environment in 1998, to facilitate the privatization exercise that commenced later that year. Work on Highway 407 West also stopped completely. Nothing more happened until it, too, was rolled into the privatization exercise.

This signaled the end of the major decision making phases. Political direction to accelerate Highway 407 as a toll road had been given and the civil servants had carried out that directive. The partnership had been scaled down, with the government now financing the highway through the OTCC, rather than having the private sector handle this part of the project as well. Still, the government would not have to subsidize the highway. The contract to design and deliver the highway had been awarded to a consortium. There had been some controversy around the announcement. Yet, even though the government had changed shortly thereafter, none of the decisions taken by the Rae government in this matter had been altered or reversed. The project continued, though planned extensions of the highway were deferred. The next phases – building and operating the highway – were about to begin.

CHAPTER 6

FORMING A MANAGEMENT TEAM

The Rae Government had already demonstrated its willingness to adopt unconventional – even unprecedented – approaches to the Highway 407 project. This willingness continued into the implementation phase. Rather than give responsibility to MTO, it established a Crown corporation, the Ontario Transportation Capital Corporation (OTCC), to take primary responsibility for overseeing development.[1] This chapter, therefore, focuses on OTCC, and we discuss its establishment, responsibilities, operations, and governance. We also deal with the recruitment of a CEO and the financing of the project.

CREATION OF THE OTCC

While the Highway 407 project was being developed, the government took steps to create a Crown corporation to administer it. OTCC would report to the Minister of Transportation but be separate from MTO. The intent was to remove it from the bureaucracy of the ministry and to create a streamlined, fast-moving body that could deal effectively with a private sector partner. It would have the explicit purpose of raising capital and administering the construction of transportation infrastructure.

The OTCC was initially envisaged as a small, specialized group of no more than 12 professional staff, with expertise in administering contracts and in financial issues. Technical expertise would be borrowed from MTO as needed. Minister Pouliot was insistent that the OTCC should not develop into a large bureaucracy. He was generally wary of empire building in the public service and was determined that this not happen at the OTCC. Pouliot therefore proposed that OTCC be established as a Schedule 4 Crown corporation, which would give it the following characteristics:

- A service delivery mandate working in partnership with the private sector

- Financial self-sufficiency, operating outside the consolidated revenue fund

- Staff appointments within the Ontario Public Service.

The appointment regime would give its staff flexibility to move back and forth into other government positions. This averted any labour issues when the corporation was formed.

OPPOSITION FROM THE MINISTRY OF FINANCE

From the outset, the Ministry of Finance showed little enthusiasm for a corporation with the ability to approach the financial markets independently. Like most central agencies, it was uncomfortable with decentralizing power to other parts of the government. It jealously guarded the role of raising capital for itself and resented what it perceived as the usurpation of its powers. MTO staff prepared a draft policy paper on the OTCC and circulated it to the relevant ministries. Despite several follow up requests, there was no response from the Ministry of Finance for several months. Finally, after more prodding from the Premier's Office, Finance agreed with the underlying principles of the OTCC.

The OTCC was to be created under the Capital Investment Plan Act, which the Minister of Finance would present to the Legislature. The Act would also create the Ontario Financing Authority, a Crown corporation reporting to the Minister of Finance and responsible for managing Ontario's public debt.[2] Finance was expected to work with MTO's draft as far as the OTCC portion of the proposed legislation went. Typically, Finance gave no indication of any changes it would make in a draft plan until the last minute, a tactic no doubt intended to prevent rebuttal by the agency authoring the draft.

The submission seeking approval for the Capital Investment Plan Act was to be presented to P&P in November 1993. P&P usually met on a Monday afternoon. In the late morning of the scheduled meeting day, Finance was finally ready to brief MTO on the submission. Barbara Stewart, a director at Finance, briefed senior MTO personnel, including Deputy Minister George Davies, ADM for Policy and Planning David Guscott, Director of Investment Strategy Tony Salerno and Chandran Mylvaganam, the Minister's Chief of Staff. To their dismay, the OTCC envisaged by Finance bore little resemblance to MTO's original concept. Under Finance's proposal, the OTCC would require the explicit approval of the Minister of Finance whenever it wanted to borrow or spend money. In effect, Finance wanted the OTCC to be treated like any other government department. Most of the benefits of an OTCC would disappear. MTO expressed their strong objections to Stewart, who agreed to take them back to her ministry's leadership. A few hours later, MTO was informed by Finance that they intended to proceed to P&P without incorporating any of MTO's suggestions.

MTO immediately briefed the Premier's policy advisers on the situation and the possible consequences for the OTCC. When P&P considered the issue that afternoon, the Premier, followed by other members of P&P, quickly attacked Finance's proposal. No one spoke up in support of Finance's position. The Minister of Finance, Floyd Laughren, who apparently had not been made aware of MTO's concerns, remained silent, while the Deputy Minister of Finance at the time, Eleanor Clitheroe, also said nothing. Participants at the meeting considered it one of the most remarkable they had witnessed for the vehemence of the criticism and the absence of any ministerial defence. The result was that P&P reinstated the key elements of MTO's model of the OTCC's powers. It directed that legislation establishing the OTCC be drawn up to reflect this.

As a consequence, the Capital Investment Plan Act (Revised Statutes of Ontario 1993, chapter 23) specified that OTCC's powers include "providing financing for transportation programs and projects and facilitating the development and implementation of such programs and projects" [section 39.1] and "mak[ing] agreements for the planning, design, financing, construction, improvement, operation, maintenance, leasing or acquisition of a highway, public transportation project or other transportation project." [section 40.1.a]. The government gave OTCC broad powers to be involved in the construction of new toll highways, financing capital transfers to municipal transit authorities and GO Transit, and advising the province and municipalities on transit policy, investment, and operations.

COMPOSITION OF THE OTCC

The government had intended the OTCC to have a mixed board of directors, with members from the bureaucracy and the private sector. At this point, the board consisted entirely of public servants. The government, primarily because of inertia, had yet to appoint the external directors. Responsibility for nominating directors for approval by Premier Rae belonged to the Minister of Transportation. Minister Pouliot's office had not begun the process of searching for qualified candidates. There was debate about whether the majority of the board should be drawn from the public service or outside it. The legislation creating the board was loose enough to permit either choice. The argument advanced by the bureaucracy was that having a majority of public servants was the only way the minister could be assured the board would follow his direction. Some unpleasant experiences with boards of directors of other crown corporations convinced the government that this would be prudent. Three external directors would be added to the four directors drawn from the Ontario Public Service (the CEO of OTCC; George Davies, the Deputy Minister of Transportation; David Guscott, the Assistant Deputy Minister of Transportation for Policy and Planning, and Jay Kaufman, the Deputy Minister of Finance).[3] The Deputy Minister of Transportation would chair the board.

In November 1994, at the urging of the Public Appointments Secretariat, a concerted effort was made to seek the three external board members. The government needed candidates who would give the OTCC credibility, especially in the financial markets. It also wanted to avoid any suggestion that people were appointed purely because of political affiliations. An election was expected in 1995 and re-election seemed very unlikely. The government wanted to ensure that the OTCC would continue to function smoothly in the event of an electoral defeat. Ideally, the appointees would have financial or public policy expertise. Candidates with financial backgrounds not currently working for large financial institutions were preferred, as those institutions would be disqualified from participating in any of the OTCC's borrowing. Potential candidates were identified and interviewed. Minister Pouliot nominated two retired senior executives of investment banks, George Michals and J. Michael Scott, and Sandford Borins, a professor of public management who had published papers on road pricing.[4]

The Premier's Office raised a concern about the appointments. All the appointees were Caucasian males. This was inconsistent with the government's commitment to, and strong advocacy of, employment equity. However, it accepted the minister's argument that it was not possible to find suitable, qualified candidates with the necessary financial experience and expertise from what had been designated as target groups (women, visible minorities, native Canadians, persons with disabilities). The problem was that only former executives could be considered, so as to avoid future conflicts of interest. Unfortunately, members of these target groups had only in the recent past begun to attain senior positions and had not yet reached a point of retirement. On May 15, 1995 Premier Rae appointed Michals, Scott, and Borins to the Board of the OTCC. Their appointments were for three-year terms, the typical duration of public appointments.

The selection of a CEO was made early in 1995. There was a strong view within the political side of government that the CEO should come from outside the OPS, as it was looking for what it loosely characterized as "private sector mentality" at the helm of the corporation. This was a disappointment to some of the senior staff at MTO who had been eying the position.

An executive search firm was retained to identify possible candidates. The candidate ultimately hired was Dennis Galange, a Canadian holding a CA and MBA, with experience in corporate finance, previously chief financial officer with a transportation logistics company based in Belgium. For Galange, the principal attraction of the position, as discussed in his meetings with Deputy Minister George Davies, was the shift to strategic management entailed by this position, and the possibility of involvement in a wide range of transportation projects. These included both public transit and real estate development on provincially-owned highway corridors.

As noted earlier, the OTCC had been envisaged as a streamlined organization. When it was decided to finance the highway through the OTCC, it was clear that it would have to become larger, increasing to a staff of approximately 40. Most of this increase was effected by transferring staff from within the OPS. Tony Salerno, who had been Director of Investment Strategy at MTO, came to OTCC as Executive Vice President. (He soon left OTCC, however, to become President of the Ontario Financing Authority.) Michael Cautillo, who had been involved in developing the highway since its inception in 1992, joined as Assistant Vice President and, after Salerno's departure, became Vice President for Operations and Policy. David Garner, a senior engineer in MTO, came in to run the engineering and construction aspects of the project. The legal staff was also made up of public servants on secondment. Delcan Associates, a firm of consulting engineers who had belonged to the ORDC consortium, was hired as OTCC's agent to oversee design and construction.

To emphasize its separation from the bureaucracy, OTCC located its offices in Toronto's financial district, rather than near Queen's Park or MTO's head office in suburban Downsview.

OTCC'S OPERATIONS

OTCC held monthly board meetings, usually in its offices, and occasionally at Highway 407 facilities. The board heard reports from the CEO and senior staff examining such topics as progress on construction and tolling technology, negotiations with contractors, risk management, marketing, finance, and, increasingly as the highway moved to completion, privatization. The board had an audit committee consisting of directors with accounting expertise, both public servants and external appointees, who reviewed the corporation's quarterly statements. The board gave policy direction to OTCC, while the CEO and senior staff provided day-to-day management. While the CEO reported to the Deputy Minister of Transportation through the board, of which the latter was chair, the two also had an informal reporting relationship, and were in contact more frequently when the project faced a crisis, as will be discussed in Chapter 7.

The three external directors appointed by Premier Rae were retained by the Harris government. Harris soon appointed two additional external directors, Richard Zimmerman, a lawyer with substantial experience representing the trucking industry, and Christopher Henley, a venture capitalist with experience advising public and private sector clients about infrastructure and privatization. The latter two appointments reflect a concern on the new government's part about trucking industry reaction to a toll highway and interest in privatization once the highway was built and operating.

OTCC differed from the traditional model of Crown corporation governance, in which the board meets infrequently – at most quarterly – and is chosen for party loyalty or diversity. This board met frequently and was more actively involved in oversight of management. Board decisions were consensual, in that recorded votes were almost always unanimous, without any evidence of splits between the public servants and the external directors. Thus the concern initially expressed by the bureaucracy about a board with an external majority (five of nine directors), proved unfounded. Because the government was the sole shareholder, the Minister of Transportation, acting for the government, could issue directives to OTCC, and did exercise that power on several occasions, as will be discussed in chapter 7 regarding investments to enhance safety. The fact that the minister – who was not a member of the board – could issue binding directives to the board meant that the external directors occasionally saw themselves as advisers to the minister, speaking to him through the deputy minister.

While its legal status was that of a Crown corporation, OTCC had many of the characteristics of a service agency, such as the Canadian Customs and Revenue Agency (CCRA), or what in the UK are referred to as Next Steps agencies (Zussman 2002, 65). It was given substantial managerial and financial autonomy to complete a special project. Its CEO was recruited externally. OTCC's CEO reported directly to the deputy minister, either formally at the board or informally on a day-to-day basis. Legislation, corporate by-laws, and a memorandum of agreement between the minister and the deputy minister, in his capacity as chair of the board, outlined OTCC's responsibilities. Like CCRA's Board of Management, OTCC had external representatives on its board of directors. Thus, OTCC could be considered part of the trend towards "agentification," the establishment of agencies with increased autonomy responsible for special projects or service-oriented functions, operating within the framework of ministerial government (Pollitt and Bouckaert 2000, 77-86, 165-6).

FINANCING HIGHWAY 407

Financing the highway was a major concern for OTCC's staff and its board. Because the project was intended to be self-financing, it was essential to minimize the cost of capital. Having both revenues and costs, Highway 407 was therefore different from a traditional public sector project. Financing decisions called upon the expertise of the staff and board, as well as the advice of the Ontario Financing Authority (OFA).

The cabinet's decision to finance Highway 407 by government rather than private sector borrowing was implemented by the OFA. OTCC paid its contractors from short-term (30-90 day) loans from OFA. These loans, in turn, were financed by OFA's short-term borrowing at the going rate on the capital markets.

By late 1995 the board came to view this approach as fraught with risk. Short-term interest rates rose from the 5 to 6 % range in 1994 to 8 to 9 % in early to mid-1995. The project's internal rate of return[5] was then estimated at approximately 10 %, so that rising interest rates threatened its economic viability. Both short and long term rates declined in summer and fall 1995, which led OTCC to consider converting a substantial portion of its debt from short to long term to provide some stability. But in mid-October, the board was told by OFA that the capital markets were unwilling to make any long-term loans to Ontario (or, for that matter, other Canadian governments) because of the Quebec referendum that would be held on October 30.

After the narrow victory on the "no" side in the referendum, the capital markets resumed financing the Canadian public sector's long-term debt. The unavailability of long-term capital because of referendum-generated uncertainty deeply concerned the board; as a consequence, soon after the referendum it resolved that the Deputy Minister of Transportation would approach the Deputy Minister of Finance to authorize OFA to borrow on OTCC's behalf up to $600 million for up to 30 years. This required careful arranging of priorities because both the province and Ontario Hydro were also borrowing. In December, OFA issued a 30-year debenture of $500 million at 8.25 % (with an effective interest rate of 8.52 % after $14 million in financing costs) to cover OTCC's accumulated debt to that point.

In the following two years, short-term rates declined dramatically, from 8 % in fall 1995 to 3.5 % in mid-1997. Long-term rates also declined, but not nearly as much. As a consequence, OTCC funded additional payments to contractors by short-term borrowing. OTCC staff, the board of directors, and representatives of OFA periodically discussed whether to convert more short-term debt to long-term, but chose to stay short-term. By spring 1998, when short-term rates had increased somewhat from the lows of the previous year, OTCC had accumulated over $900 million in short-term (30-60 day) debt at an average cost of slightly less than 5 %. As a result, OTCC's average cost of borrowing at that time, taking into account both its $900 million in short-term debt and its $500 million in 30 year debentures, was 6 %. This compared favourably with the project's projected internal rate of return of 10 % and the average cost of borrowing of 7 % in its plans.

Thus the financing strategy evolved from OTCC's initial risk-aversion, shifting from borrowing long-term to protect against rising interest rates that would threaten the project's financial viability to an acceptance of greater risk by taking advantage of falling short-term interest rates to improve the project's financial performance. External appointees and public servants on the board as well as the Ontario Financing Authority were all supportive of this financing strategy.

We have seen how OTCC dealt with the financial risks involved in the Highway 407 project. In the next chapter, we turn to two other sources of risk, the safety of the highway's design and the effectiveness of its technology.

CHAPTER 7

DELIVERING THE HIGHWAY

By mid-1995, most of the pieces were in place to deliver the highway. OTCC had its full complement of staff and was overseeing the project. The construction contract had been signed, and the CHIC consortium was building the road. The technology contract had not yet been signed with the Bell, Bell Sygma, and Hughes Aircraft consortium, but it was clear the consortium and OTCC were moving to an agreement. The Harris government, which took office in June 1995, accepted the rationale for the highway and the use of tolling, and made no attempt to change the construction contract signed by the Rae government. The one difference between the NDP and the Conservatives on the project was that the Conservatives did not accept the NDP's ambitious plan for OTCC: involvement in transportation financing, policy development, construction of other toll roads, and the development of transportation corridor lands. As a consequence, OTCC's role was restricted to overseeing the development of Highway 407. Responsibility for any development of corridor lands was given to the Ontario Realty Corporation. This caused some dismay among OTCC staff, particularly CEO Dennis Galange, who had looked forward to OTCC involvement in all these areas. The development of Highway 407 nevertheless turned out to be sufficiently challenging to keep OTCC staff fully occupied.

An important managerial change occurred in mid-November 1996, with the replacement of George Davies by Jan Rush as Deputy Minister of Transportation and Chair of the OTCC Board. Prior to this appointment, Rush was Assistant Deputy Minister for Policy, and Secretary to the Policy and Priorities Board in Cabinet Office. She had trained as a transportation economist and worked in MTO previously, so she was well aware of the issues involved. She arrived just in time to assume primary responsibility for advising the minister on managing the issues discussed in this chapter.

In narratives about project management – as in many other areas of life – the most interesting part of the story is not what went well, but rather what didn't. It is the problems, sometimes unanticipated, that had to be solved to deliver the project that usually prove most instructive. Two such problems on the Highway 407 project ultimately assumed crisis proportions for the government and posed significant management challenges. The first concerned safety, in particular, public allegations that OTCC's contractors had sacrificed driver safety to reduce costs; the second concerned technology, specifically the consortium's failure to complete the electronic tolling technology by the promised date.

SAFETY

Throughout 1995 and 1996, the roadwork component of the project was moving ahead smoothly, within budget and slightly ahead of schedule. It appeared that the road would be ready to open in fall 1996, or by year's end at the latest. As a consequence, OTCC stepped up its marketing campaign. The agreement with CHIC included a possible bonus for early completion, and CHIC ultimately received a bonus of $6 million. (Delays were becoming apparent with the technology, as will be discussed in the next section of this chapter; nevertheless, it was feasible to open the highway before the tolling system was operational.)

On October 15, 1996, Provincial Auditor Erik Peters released his annual report, which included a chapter on OTCC. The main criticisms advanced were that the government might have received more bids for the project by unbundling its three components (construction, tolling, maintenance) and that because the government had accepted all the risk of financing the entire project itself, a public-private partnership was not established. With respect to value engineering, the audit noted that OTCC was able to save an estimated $300 million by deferring or deleting some interchanges and "changing the standards normally applied to highway construction." As discussed in chapter 4, an example of such changes was reducing the length of merging lanes from 500 metres to 446 metres — the standard before the province converted from Imperial to metric measurement. The auditor recommended that the ministry assess the applicability of the revised standards originating from the Highway 407 value engineering exercise as benchmarks for cost reductions on other highway projects (Provincial Auditor 1996, 236-50).

The auditor's report did not attract much public attention. When it was discussed for the first time in the legislature's Standing Committee on Public Accounts on October 17, Highway 407 was mentioned just twice, both times in relation to financing, rather than construction standards or safety (Hansard 1996b).[1] The initial discussion in the public accounts committee clearly revealed the political alignment regarding Highway 407. The NDP, which had initiated the project, was siding with the government in support of it, and only the Liberals were probing for weaknesses.

The Toronto Star, which focuses on Toronto news and which traditionally supports the Liberals, was also looking critically at the highway. On Tuesday, November 12, reporter Bob Mitchell published a front-page article headlined "Police Fear Toll Highway will be a Killer: Head-on Crashes Certain, they say" (Mitchell 1996a). The main police criticisms reported were that the highway's grassy median strips did not have centre rails and that no protective barriers were placed around its 30-metre-high light standards. The article was based on interviews with OPP officers, including Len Briden, a traffic staff sergeant who had retired the previous year. According to the article, "Briden and several other OPP officers expressed their concerns when they met with officials of Canadian Highways International Corporation" [but] "'nobody ever sought any input from the front line officers as to what we thought about the design,' Briden said."

The Committee on Public Accounts had scheduled a meeting on November 21 to discuss the chapter of the auditor's report dealing with Highway 407. Two days prior, Bob Mitchell published another article in *The Toronto Star* on Highway 407 (Mitchell 1996b). Featured on the front page, it carried the banner headline "Highway 407 safety rules lowered: report" and showed a large photograph of provincial auditor Peters, in his fall coat, standing at an on-ramp to Highway 407, holding his open report. The article opened sensationally enough: "Safety standards for Highway 407 were lowered to save taxpayers $300 million, the provincial auditor's report says. The province 'departed from ministry standards' for highway construction when approving the contract, auditor Erik Peters agreed in an interview yesterday" (Mitchell 1996b). Later in the article, on the back page of the front section, Mitchell qualified his charges: "Peters said he didn't use the word 'safety' in his report, which is to be reviewed Thursday by the public accounts committee. He said because he isn't an engineer, he couldn't 'make judgments on what is dangerous and what isn't'" (Mitchell 1996b).

Peters took a similar line at the Committee hearing. Jack Carroll, a Conservative member, started the discussion by asking Peters, "Was it your intention in evaluating the Highway 407 project to make any recommendations or any comments on safety? If in fact it was, what expertise did you use to come up with those comments about safety?" Peters replied, "That's a very quick and good answer: I'm not an expert.

I therefore did not make any comments about safety. None of the comments that we make in the report nor comments that we made to the media were about compromised safety. To the best of my knowledge, the only safety concerns were raised by the OPP, but they were not raised by my office" (Hansard 1996c, 5).

The headline and the photograph spoke louder than Peters's disclaimers, either in the original article in *The Toronto Star* or at the Committee on Public Accounts. Two authoritative voices — the OPP and the auditor — had raised doubts in the public mind about the safety of the highway. Though OTCC staff had prepared a refutation of the concerns raised by OPP officers and the provincial auditor, the politicians decided not to stonewall. On November 20, the day before the committee hearing, Premier Harris announced that Highway 407 would not be opened until the Ontario government was assured that it was safe, and Transport Minister Al Palladini announced that he would appoint an independent third-party investigator to examine safety concerns (Walker and Girard 1996).

One other facet of this story emerged in *The Toronto Star* a few days later. On November 29, Bob Mitchell published a story entitled "Province excluded in Highway 407 inspections" (Mitchell 1996c). The story quoted Wayne Hagerty, vice-president of Ontario Public Service Employees' Union (OPSEU) local 536, who complained that provincial highway inspectors were not allowed to inspect construction quality for Highway 407, despite having that responsibility for the work of other private contractors. The article also noted that many of the inspectors, including Hagerty, were being laid off at the end of November.

The safety episode provides a perfect example of the informal yet highly effective process by which a collation may form to oppose a major government project. The political opposition – in this case, the Liberals – and the newspaper most closely allied with the Liberals, *The Toronto Star*, took the lead. A marginalized interest group – in this case, rank and file OPP officers and highway inspectors who felt excluded from the development of the highway – seized the opportunity thus provided to go on the public record with their concerns. The highway was not being built on the honour system – as the inspectors alleged – but their normal role was given to an independent agent, a construction consulting company under contract to OTCC. If the OPP had concerns about a highway being built in the traditional way, they would have directed them to MTO. It appears that OPP officers did not know where to raise safety concerns for Highway 407. *The Toronto Star* article reported that they approached the contractor. In testimony to the public accounts committee, David Garner, OTCC executive vice-president for engineering, said that he found no formal written concerns raised by the OPP regarding safety. He did recall a meeting with the OPP at the project office in which one of the officers asked whether the highway would have median barriers, and "it was pointed out that the provincial standard did not require median barriers and it was felt that the issue was closed at that point" (Hansard 1996c, 10). But clearly the issue was not closed in the minds of all OPP officers.

The key player in the coalition, however, turned out to be Provincial Auditor Erik Peters. He was looking for the media attention that his report did not receive when it was first released. By allowing *The Toronto Star* to photograph him beside the highway, he gave credence to its claim that the highway would be unsafe. The front-page photograph and the headline were the real story, not the Auditor's disclaimers published on page 24. After the story appeared, the Auditor's staff told officials at OTCC that the Auditor felt he had been manipulated by *The Toronto Star*, and that he was embarrassed by the story. By then, of course, the damage had been done.

With front-page, scare headlines and the auditor's involvement, Premier Harris and Transportation Minister Palladini had little choice but to act to allay public concerns. Road safety was very much a "hot button" issue following a number of incidents involving tires coming off transport trucks, causing serious accidents and loss of life. Palladini had taken ownership of the safety issue and launched a vigorous truck inspection campaign (Hansard 1996a, 68-76, 82-94). Ignoring safety concerns raised about Highway 407 would have appeared inconsistent, if not hypocritical. Once defined as a safety issue, it came within the purview of MTO, and Palladini took control. He established the terms of reference for the safety review, and the committee would report to him, not to OTCC. OTCC's day-to-day operating autonomy was trumped by ministerial action.

Minister Palladini asked the Professional Engineers of Ontario (PEO), the regulatory body for engineers in Ontario, to "review whether appropriate engineering standards were used in Highway 407 and determine if safety was compromised in the design and construction of the highway" (Palladini 1996). PEO established a six-person expert committee to review the highway, with access to all documentation, and a two-month time frame to report. At the outset, the committee amended its terms of reference to state that it would "consider whether there are seemingly cost-effective opportunities to enhance the safety of the highway which merit consideration by the Ministry of Transport." The committee reviewed all the documentation, inspected the highway, met with all interested parties, including the OPP, and reported on April 4, 1997 (Professional Engineers of Ontario 1997b).

The committee concluded that generally Highway 407 was built to current standards for 400-series highways, but it recommended a number of modifications to improve on current standards. The report was critical of the value engineering process, concluding that "no explicit consideration of safety was evident in the value engineering exercise for Highway 407 – it was only a cost-cutting exercise." The committee also recommended better cooperation and sharing of safety information and expertise between MTO and the OPP. With respect to the road itself, the committee recommended modifications such as installing crash cushions (i.e. sand-filled barrels) around high mast lighting poles and bridge supports, reshaping the highway's shoulders, improving signage, and installing rumble strips. Significantly, it did not accept the OPP officers' recommendation of a median barrier, because the width of the median met current standards and because the barriers themselves could become a hazard (Professional Engineers of Ontario 1997a).

Senior public servants were very disappointed by the engineers' recommendations, which they felt were predicated on the notion that safety was an absolute that should not be traded off against any other value. They also felt the recommendations were intended to push the government to exceed its current safety standards, without making a case as to why current standards should be exceeded. The recommendations were studied in detail by a joint MTO-OTCC team. On May 1, Transportation Minister Palladini announced that he was accepting all the PEO expert committee's recommendations, which would involve a cost of between $13 and $15 million and take a month to complete (Mitchell 1997a). He directed the OTCC board to authorize the work and to pay for it out of the contingency fund of $45 million. Again, given the position he had taken on other safety issues, it would have been politically difficult for Palladini not to accept these recommendations. Had the engineers recommended building a median barrier, the minister would have faced a dilemma. The barrier would have been very expensive and would have required almost three months to install. It would have also created pressure to install barriers on median strips on all the other 400 series highways.

Highway 407 would be ready for traffic in early June. The tolling system would not. It was becoming increasingly difficult, however, to keep drivers, cyclists, skateboarders, inline skaters, and even pedestrians off a 36 kilometre highway that was ready for use.

TECHNOLOGY

Implementing electronic tolling technology proved to be the most difficult challenge faced by OTCC. The corporation was attempting to do something unprecedented – to build an all-electronic toll road integrating transponder and videoimaging technologies, with both operating at high volumes. Earlier electronic toll roads, such as California's State Highway 91, were restricted to drivers with transponders. On those roads, videoimaging was used for enforcement by capturing license plates of cars that did not have transponders. In the case of Highway 407, transponders were not mandatory for cars and videoimaging would be used for the large number of drivers who would not obtain them.

With the technology being provided by a consortium, extensive inter-organizational coordination was required, and this emerged as a second implementation challenge. The members of the consortium were originally brought together by MTO to be part of the ORDC proposal. While the CHIC proposal was chosen for the road, the tolling team allied with ORDC was chosen for the tolling technology. The members of the technology consortium included Hughes Aircraft, responsible for videoimaging, Bell Sygma, responsible for systems integration, Bell Canada, responsible for billing, and Mark IV Industries, responsible for supplying transponders. Senior public servants in MTO observed that the tolling consortium was an awkward partnership at the outset, and that, throughout the project, its members were continually squabbling and devoting considerable energy to protecting their respective legal positions in the event the technology failed.

OTCC's role was to monitor its contractors and manage the risks. It did this in a number of ways. At the request of the external directors, staff presented a risk assessment and risk management report at every meeting. They identified five major categories of risks – tolling technology, highway usage, construction, financing, and enforcement – and listed all the individual risks they could think of under each category. (An example of tolling risk would be the circulation of counterfeit transponders; one of usage risk would be a failure to achieve an acceptable level of transponder usage.) For each risk, staff estimated the probability it would occur, described its consequences, and developed a contingency plan for dealing with it. This risk assessment approach was a useful way of thinking about and managing risk; for example, staff or the board could identify and discuss the "top ten" risks or track the evolution of specific risks.

The members of the technology consortium were monitored very closely by OTCC staff. The toll system supply agreement – a contract worth approximately \$53.4 million – was signed on September 15, 1995.[2] Immediately thereafter, the contractors began providing weekly progress reports to OTCC staff. As a consequence, there were few surprises, and OTCC quickly saw when there were problems. Because of the strained relations among the firms, OTCC staff often dealt with them separately, rather than having one report on behalf of the others.

Videoimaging itself was not the main difficulty. During winter 1995-96, Hughes Aircraft quietly mounted a camera at the interchange of Highways 400 and 401 and took a sample of several thousand images of rear license plates under a variety of weather conditions. This real-life experiment demonstrated the technology was working reliably. The problems lay in processing the videoimages. Each car had to be captured when it entered the highway and when it left. To ensure that the license plate was captured, a videoimage included the entire back end of the automobile, so it took up a substantial amount of computer capacity. The entire file of videoimages had to be sorted continuously to match the two images of every one of the thousands of cars without transponders using the highway every day. Pairs of matched videoimages produced records of trips by automobiles, which then had to be compared with MTO's motor vehicle database to produce bills. Transponders were easier to work with, because transponder records required less computer capacity than videoimages, were virtually always accurate, and presented no difficulty matching records. The entire operation required substantial computer capacity, at a time when capacity was not yet as plentiful or inexpensive as it is now. The consequences of having too little capacity were critical: if the capacity demanded by the file of videoimages exceeded the system's storage capacity, the system would crash and all the unsorted videoimages would be lost.

The deadlines in the contract were for tolling to be operational for drivers with transponders by December 31, 1996 and for full tolling to be operational by March 31, 1997. While progress reports were showing slippage by March 1996, by fall it was apparent that the deadlines would be missed. George Davies frequently and sometimes urgently called presidents and vice-presidents of the consortium members. When Jan Rush took over as deputy minister, she quickly summoned senior managers of the consortium to outline the seriousness of the government's concern about missing deadlines, and asked them what they were going to do to restore the government's confidence. The board also met with the contractors to emphasize the extent of their dissatisfaction. In the case of the meeting with the board, staff prepared a detailed set of questions. The message that the deputy minister, the board, and OTCC staff conveyed was that they expected the firms in the consortium – at their own expense – to mobilize additional resources to meet their obligations, which they eventually did. This often involved increasing the number of staff working on the project. One of the issues the project had to contend with was a shortage of COBOL programmers, many of whom were already being used to deal with the "millennium bug".[3]

The technology problems came to the fore in November and December 1996, at precisely the same time the safety issue was raised. The fact that the technology was behind schedule contributed to Minister Palladini's immediate willingness to launch a safety review. Delaying the opening of the road for safety reasons would permit more time to resolve the technology problems (Walker and Girard 1996). At that point, OTCC began contingency planning for the possibility that the integrated technology could not be made to work. Options considered included restricting the highway to cars with transponders or charging a flat rate based on only one videoimage, thus eliminating the computer problem of reading and matching two images for each car.

There were two additional sources of pressure on the consortium. As of January 1, 1997, they began paying monthly penalties for missing deadlines. (Ultimately, they paid almost $1 million in penalties.) More importantly, missing deadlines reflected upon their reputation and compromised potential sales of this technology elsewhere. Because the tolling technology represented a leading-edge development, the attention of transport agencies throughout the world was focused on whether it could be made to work.

When the road was ready in June 1997, following the safety modifications, Minister Palladini decided to open it. Given his background as owner of a very successful automobile dealership, he was deeply interested in marketing the highway. He saw the fact that the road was ready before the technology as an opportunity, not a problem. The toll-free period would provide an opportunity to attract drivers who might have avoided the highway if tolls were in place. They might continue to use the road after the tolls were imposed.

The opening of Highway 407 on June 7, 1997 for free use, however, exacerbated the technology problem. Because no fees were being charged, traffic on the highway was over 300,000 vehicles per day, rather than the anticipated 100,000 per day with tolls. The uncertainty about when tolls would be implemented created no incentive for drivers to obtain transponders. Every time the consortium attempted to run the tolling system live, its capacity to process videoimages was immediately swamped during morning rush hour, and the system crashed. OTCC adopted a risk-averse position: it would not charge tolls until it was certain it had enough capacity to process transponder and videoimaging records for the traffic levels experienced during the free use period. Consequently, OTCC decided to spend an additional $13 million to double videoimaging capacity, which would take several weeks to install. This approach was criticized by the media as being unduly cautious (Barber 1997, Corcoran 1997, Gombu and Wilkes 1997, Mitchell 1997b, Mitchell 1997c). Within the OTCC board, there was growing impatience with the delay and growing pressure to adopt one of the fallback alternatives.

The consortium was finally able to show that its integrated technology could track over 300,000 vehicles per day, approximately half of which were not using transponders. Highway 407 went into operation as a toll road on Thanksgiving Day, Monday, October 14. As predicted, the traffic level fell to 100,000 cars per day. Almost immediately 50 percent of the drivers began using transponders, and the technology worked. Virtually all vehicles using transponders, and well over 80 percent of those being videoimaged, were captured by the tolling system. The highway had been delivered.

The minister, senior MTO staff, and OTCC staff all breathed a huge collective sigh of relief and felt they had won a major victory. The government had borne the capital, technology, and market risks for the project. The various contingency plans and fallback options had not been required. There had been substantial public, media, and political skepticism and criticism – especially when the project was delayed – about the technology, which had ultimately been proven wrong. Finally, because the technology worked and the highway was collecting revenue, the capital markets would not move Ontario's borrowing for Highway 407 from off-book status to regular public debt.

THE NEXT STEPS

There was little opportunity, however, to savour this victory. There was much to be done in terms of enhancing the technology and extending the highway in the west and the east. On two occasions, the computer system came close to crashing; as a consequence, the consortium kept adding additional processing capacity.

After opening the first 36-kilometre stage of highway, traffic volumes and corresponding revenues grew. Construction continued on the remaining section and all 69 kilometres were completed by September 4, 1998 (see map on page 49). Plans to construct the highway eastward beyond its terminus at Markham Road, however, were at least temporarily suspended by the Harris government, even though the environmental assessment had been completed for the 15 kilometre section between Markham Road and Brock Road in Pickering. This created a problem that had been anticipated. Markham Road (provincial highway 48) was a busy north-south artery. If Highway 407 ended there, traffic would be dumped onto this highway, clogging it. As a consequence, the highway was opened only up to McCowan Road in the east and the four kilometre section to Markham Road remained closed, even though it had been completed.

The Rae government had always planned further easterly construction commencing before the central portion of Highway 407, which terminated at Markham Road, was completed. It was expected that this would relieve pressure on Markham Road. Don Cousens, the Mayor of Markham since 1994 and former Conservative MPP for that area, had continued to support the construction plans for Highway 407 because of this undertaking by the Rae government. The inaction of the Harris government created a problem for Cousens. Similarly, the senior civil servants at MTO, who had shepherded the first stage of Highway 407 to successful completion, would have liked to press on with the rest of the highway as previously envisaged, but because of the prior controversies hesitated to be viewed as advocates by the Harris government.

Traffic volumes on Highway 407 grew steadily. The average number of weekday trips in October 1997 was 102,668. By February 1999, this had risen to 204,840. The highway was an undisputed success. It was given an asset value of $1.5 billion on the government's balance sheets. The government had not utilized the OTCC as originally envisaged, however, to further develop ancillary revenue opportunities in the corridor. Work on the eastern and western extensions was also in doubt, and the four kilometre segment between McCowan Rd and Markham Rd was completed, but unopened. Thus, development of Highway 407 was at a standstill when the Harris government began to consider privatization, which is the subject of the next chapter.

CHAPTER 8

PRIVATIZATION AND ITS AFTERMATH: POLITICS, IDEOLOGY, AND CONFRONTATION

PRIVATIZATION AND THE CONSERVATIVE GOVERNMENT

The Harris government had been elected on a platform – the Common Sense Revolution – that promised at least implicitly to privatize vast swathes of government operations. Crown corporations such as the Liquor Control Board of Ontario (LCBO) and TV Ontario, as well as Ontario Hydro were seen as prime candidates. Yet, the government moved very slowly to set up a mechanism to systematically examine privatization prospects. In 1996, Rob Sampson, an MPP from Mississauga, was appointed minister without portfolio with responsibility for privatization. A Cabinet Committee on Privatization (CCOP) was also created, but Sampson was merely a member. The chair was Finance Minister Ernie Eves. A Privatization Secretariat was also created and Paul Currie, a former senior partner from Coopers and Lybrand, was brought in as CEO in early 1997. Ninety percent of the staff were on contract from the private sector, with the remaining 10 % drawn from the OPS.

Like the staff at the Secretariat, Sampson was strongly committed to privatization, but it was soon evident where the real decision-making power lay. Whenever Sampson brought forward a case for privatization of a major corporation, Eves would reject it. Eves was much more politically astute than the less experienced Sampson, with a corresponding sense of the value of friendships and loyalty. Andy Brandt, Eves' former colleague in the legislature and interim leader of the Conservatives, chaired the LCBO. Its employees had also waged an effective media campaign suggesting that privatized liquor sales would result in unchecked sales of alcohol to teenagers by vendors who were only interested in making a profit. Eves realized that this had created serious public concern. The LCBO, clearly, would not be privatized.

Despite rumours of potential disappointment, an army of consultants and investment bankers eagerly awaited Sampson's first announcement on candidates for privatization. When it was made in April 1997, none of the major corporations was on the list. The highlight was two tree nurseries for immediate privatization and a few other entities for study. Highway 407 was not mentioned.

The "revolution" was moving forward on other fronts however. A government task force, chaired by Bob Wood, the MPP for London South, had been mandated to review agencies, boards, and commissions. It issued a report in early 1997, listing entities that could be sold off or abolished. The government had acted on some of these recommendations.

An election was expected in early 1999. To secure political credibility, the government wanted to show movement towards a balanced budget, while at the same time cutting taxes and boosting spending in critical sectors such as health. With a gap between revenues and planned expenditures, the pressure was growing to raise funds through the sale of assets. Only the aforementioned tree nurseries and a few aircraft belonging to Norontair, an airline which served Northern Ontario and which had been shut down by the government, had been privatized to that point, bringing in relatively little revenue and calling into question the government's commitment to privatization. Something on a much larger scale was needed. Furthermore, the government wanted to reaffirm its ideological commitment to privatization (Ministry of Transportation 2000).

In a report issued on February 18, 1998, Wood's committee identified the OTCC and thus Highway 407 as a suitable candidate for a stock offering (an initial purchase offering, or IPO) or outright privatization. Rob Sampson, the Minister for Privatization, and Tony Clement, the Minister of Transportation, announced jointly that the government would explore options for Highway 407. Countering charges that privatization would result in higher tolls on the highway, Clement and Sampson claimed that if anything, tolls would decrease because the successful bidder would want to encourage use (Mitchell, 1998). Shortly thereafter, the OTCC was alerted that it should prepare for a change in governance. The process was to be managed by the Privatization Secretariat. The government began clearing the decks in preparation for a sale. The OTCC's external directors were not reappointed when their terms ran out, commencing in early 1998.

The Privatization Secretariat retained RBC Capital Markets and Merrill Lynch as financial advisers. It was soon apparent that an IPO would take longer to put together and would in all likelihood bring in less revenue to the government than outright privatization. With the strategic imperatives of the upcoming election growing more pressing, the sale of the OTCC was put on the fast track.

THE PROCESS

The Privatization Secretariat began hiring the consultants it would need for the work. In addition to the financial advisers, PricewaterhouseCoopers was retained as process auditors and consultants, a role that their predecessor company Price Waterhouse had played in the original 407 project. The American engineering consultants Parsons Brinkerhoff and the Canadian firm Dillon Consulting became technical advisers. The ubiquitous Wilbur Smith Associates once again forecast traffic volumes and revenues and KPMG were retained as transportation policy advisers. Hiring advisers was not an easy task. Most of the bigger consulting firms had already associated themselves with the consortia that were forming to bid on the privatization. Indeed, it can be argued that the few major firms that remained outside the competition did better for themselves, as they were virtually certain to be hired by the government as advisers.

Serious work on planning the privatization began in June 1998, with the drawing up of an expression of interest (EOI) document for prospective bidders for the OTCC. It was issued in September. The EOI was explicit in the qualifications required of key personnel on a consortium's team, specifying the sizes and types of projects on which they should have experience. Consortia had to respond by November 27, 1998. The government's intent was to widen the field of bidders to include overseas as well as Canadian participants, so as to maximize the price achievable at an auction. Most of the submissions had a few gaps in the required information. Rather than disqualify anyone at this stage, consortia were therefore given an additional week to respond to questions raised by the project team about their EOI. Final responses to these questions were submitted by December 7, 1998. All four consortia that expressed interest were qualified to bid on the highway.

A change in leadership at the Privatization Secretariat took place on September 1, 1998 when Scott Carson, the Dean of the Business School at Wilfrid Laurier University, became its CEO. Carson had served on Minister Sampson's advisory board, a group of business people who advised the minister on privatization, since April 1997, when the secretariat was created. He would shepherd the privatization process through to completion.

The Privatization Secretariat would regularly seek policy direction from Minister Sampson and the CCOP. The whole cabinet would then be asked to ratify its decisions. As we will see, politicians made the ultimate decisions about both the privatization framework and the evaluation of the bids.

THE CONSORTIA

CHIC, which had designed and built Highway 407 and run it through its subsidiary Canadian Highways Management Corporation (CHMC), was one of the bidding consortia. It had teamed up with other companies to win competitions for two other toll highways - Nova Scotia's Highway 104 and the Cross-Israel (Derech Eretz) highway.[1] CHIC was generally perceived to enjoy an inherent advantage because its experience in building and operating Highway 407 gave it the type of detailed, hands-on knowledge that could not be available to its competitors. Newcourt Credit and CIBC were its financial partners in this round.

ORDC had re-formed with many of the core of companies from its team for the original bid in 1993. It had teamed with the large Spanish infrastructure company Grupo Dragados to win the bid for the Fredericton – Moncton toll highway in New Brunswick.[2] The consortium also included Infrastructure Trust of Australia, the predecessor of the Macquarie Infrastructure Group, and Borealis Infrastructure Management. The latter was partially owned by OMERS, which managed the pension fund of local government employees in Ontario.

A third consortium, later named 407 International Corporation, consisted of Cintra Concesiones de Infraestructuras de Transporte S.A. and the large Quebec-based engineering firm SNC-Lavalin. Cintra was a subsidiary of yet another Spanish construction giant with extensive toll road experience, Grupo Ferrovial. Capital D'Amérique CDPQ, a subsidiary of the Caisse de dépot et placement du Québec, was the major funding partner.

The Woodbridge Company, which was the holding company for the Thomson family, led the final consortium. Peter Kiewit Sons, who had tried unsuccessfully to qualify for the original project in 1993 was a part of this group as was Warren Paving, which had been a part of the original ORDC consortium in 1993. Goldman Sachs and the TD Bank were also members.

THE LEGISLATION

On October 19, 1998 Sampson introduced Bill 70 in the Ontario legislature. Graced with the somewhat Orwellian title, "An act to engage the private sector in improving transportation infrastructure, reducing traffic congestion, creating jobs and stimulating economic activity through the sale of Highway 407," its actual purpose was to permit the Minister for Privatization, at the direction of the cabinet, to transfer the government's interest in Highway 407 to the private sector. The first step would be to remove the OTCC from the provisions of the Capital Investment Plan Act 1993 and bring it under the Business Corporations Act. The Crown would hold all shares of the OTCC and vested the Minister for Privatization with the responsibility for selling them. Bill 70 also gave the new owners the power to levy tolls and specified that the Registrar of Motor Vehicles, an official of the Ministry of Transportation, would withhold vehicle registrations from owners of delinquent accounts. The bill had second reading on November 5, 1998 and proceeded to the Resource Development Committee of the Legislature.

Unlike the Rae government, which had consulted extensively with user groups to ensure their support, or at least to prevent opposition to the original 407 project, the Harris government settled for a single day of public hearings at the Committee. Several organizations opposed the proposed privatization. One of them, the Canadian Automobile Association, in its representation to the committee on November 19, 1998 proved notably prescient, charging that:

- The government will break its promise to limit tolls to a short time and to lift them when construction has been paid, and

- Tolls and service charges will likely rise, and if the operator is financially savvy, they may rise exorbitantly (Hansard 1998).

The legislation underwent only minor technical amendments before it was reported out of committee on November 23. It was passed by the legislature on December 10, 1998, barely a week before the end of the legislative session.

THE REQUEST FOR PROPOSALS

On December 23, 1998 an RFP was issued to the four consortia. Bidders were expected to quote the price they would pay for the highway and for the right to construct additional sections. Completion of the 24-kilometre western portion of the highway to link up with Highway 403 and the Queen Elizabeth Way (QEW) was mandatory. There were four options in the east. Under Option, 1 the highway was to extend 15 kilometres to Brock Road in Pickering. Under Option 2, it was to extend to the Ajax – Whitby border. Option 3 would take it to the Oshawa – Clarington border. Option 4 would see the highway completed, linking up with Highway 35/115 (see map on page 49). The added lengths of highway that made up options 2,3, and 4 would necessarily take longer to construct. The highway's route in this area had not been selected and the environmental assessment (EA) had not begun. Property would have to be acquired. These processes were time-consuming and potentially contentious. It could take as long as five years, by most estimates, before actual construction would begin. Such considerations did not play a part in the cabinet's decision. Indeed, people close to the process suggest that Harris and Eves either did not understand, or chose to ignore, the complexities of highway planning and construction that were dictated by legislation such as the Environmental Assessment Act.

The RFP also included a draft contract, indicating what bidders could expect their obligations to be in terms of managing the highway consistent with the public interest. These obligations were drafted by the deputy ministers' steering committee on privatization, which is discussed below.

A detailed design-build proposal for the western construction and the eastern construction under option 1 could also be submitted as a separate package, with a guaranteed maximum price. This was a fallback position for the government in the event that the bid prices for full privatization were not deemed high enough. Only consortia that had submitted privatization bids were permitted to submit design-build bids. The RFP reflected the tight timelines under which the privatization was being run. Several pages of the tender document were blank, as necessary information was not yet available. The government said this would be provided later. The initial deadline for submission of the final bids was late February. This was recognized as unreasonably tight because information that was required by the bidders was delayed. It was extended to March 28.

As in the original 407 project, the bid document prohibited discussion of the bid between members of the bidding consortia and the cabinet and this was backed by the threat of disqualification. Despite this, people associated with the bidding consortia have told us of their access to and conversations with members of the cabinet who were playing a role in the decision-making process. We discuss the possible implications at various points in this chapter and the next.

CONTENTION AND STRATEGY: THE LEASE PERIOD AND INDICATIVE BIDS

The Privatization Secretariat and its advisers had a clear preference for an outright sale of the highway. Many members of the cabinet were uncomfortable with an outright sale, however, and leaned towards a lease of the order of 35 years, a period consistent with most current practice. The consensus was that an outright sale would not be politically acceptable. The Secretariat then aimed for as long a lease period as possible. This would, in effect, simulate a sale. There were two reasons for this. The first was economic. They believed this would be the option most likely to maximize immediate revenue to the government. The second was more ideological: the Secretariat did not believe that the public sector or its agencies were capable of running a toll highway as efficiently as the private sector, which would be more likely to operate it as a business.

The cabinet, which had balked at an outright sale, seemed reluctant to enter into a long-term lease. The Secretariat consequently devised a stratagem to demonstrate that a longer lease would generate the most revenues for the government. The consortia were asked to submit non-binding indicative bids in early February, several weeks before the final bids were due. Prices were requested for lease periods of 55, 99 and 199 years. The Secretariat expected bidders to signal through this process that a longer lease period would be more attractive to them and therefore command the greatest price. This would steer the cabinet towards approving the longer lease period.

Lost in all this, however, was the fact that these indicative bids were essentially meaningless figures, which did not bind the bidders. An astute bidder, knowing the rationale behind this process, would have realized that by demonstrating in these indicative bids that the longer leases were of significantly greater value, it could influence the length of the concession period. And this indeed appears to have been the intent of the Secretariat. Once the final lease period was fixed, the consortia were free to return to more realistic bids.

While bidders were not notified that their indicative bids would be used to determine the length of the lease, at least some bidders were aware that the cabinet would see these bids. As discussed above, the authors have been told – in off-the-record interviews – that there was contact between some ministers and bidders. It is possible, therefore, that the consortia knew the real reason for the request for indicative bids. In any case, bidders tended to view this as an unnecessary "phony process." Indicative bids have sometimes been used to whittle down the number of bidders. This gives bidders an incentive to inflate their bids in the hopes of making a final short list. Even devoid of inside information, therefore, indicative bids have a tendency to be "highballed." There is also a concern that information can leak out prior to submission of final bids, further acting as a disincentive to bid realistically at this preliminary stage.

The Secretariat's strategy worked. The indicative bids reinforced its position on long-term leases and provided ammunition for the recommendation to the Cabinet Committee on Privatization and subsequently to cabinet. Still, when the CCOP's recommendation was brought to the whole cabinet, some ministers apparently questioned whether a 99-year lease was too long, though a few expressed their preference for a *199-year lease*. They were told that in the consultants' view this represented the best value for the government and since the consultants were being paid over $20 million, they should take their advice. At that point, Premier Harris ended the discussion and asked for acceptance of the recommendation. The cabinet opted for a 99-year lease. The selection of lease period was communicated to the consortia in time for them to produce their final bids.

THE STEERING COMMITTEE

While the Privatization Secretariat administered the actual privatization, a steering committee at the deputy minister level was responsible for public policy aspects including resolving the concerns and competing interests of different areas within the government. Rita Burak, the Cabinet Secretary, chaired this committee, reporting directly to the Premier. Only ministries and agencies directly affected by the privatization were on the committee – Finance, the Ontario Financing Authority, the Privatization Secretariat, Solicitor General, Attorney General, and Transportation – were represented. The OTCC was not included. Senior staff from these ministries supported the committee in its work.

Two members of the original 407 project did play roles in the privatization. Tony Salerno, who had left the OTCC in 1995 to become CEO of the OFA, sat on the steering committee. Michael Cautillo had the unique distinction of being involved with the 407 project since its inception in 1992. He had worked on the initial 407 project at MTO with Salerno. When the OTCC was formed, he moved there and became Vice President of Operations and Policy after Salerno's departure. When the OTCC was being wound down, he returned to MTO and became one of its point people on the steering committee.

There were significant differences with the 1993 contracting process. In that previous exercise, the steering committee directed all aspects of the project and made the ultimate decision about the contract. In this exercise it limited its attention to public policy issues that were not being handled by the Privatization Secretariat. Politicians made the major decisions, including the choice of the bidder. Also, some of the previous steering committee members, such as Judith Wolfson, were chosen for their particular expertise as individuals and not because their ministries were regarded as having an interest in the project.

The differing approaches reflect the different public management philosophies of the two governments. The Harris government believed there ought to be a clear separation of responsibilities between politicians and career public servants. The latter, as represented by the Steering Committee, were to confine their counsel to policy implications alone. Their roles were defined by their traditional OPS positions as representatives of their ministries. The Privatization Secretariat, drawn heavily from outside the OPS, and its private sector advisers ran the privatization itself.

The Rae government was willing to cede substantive decision-making in all areas of the process to its career civil servants. It relied on them to use their expertise and to draw on any additional resources as they saw fit to arrive at the best decision for the province, within the policy framework approved by the cabinet. The theory was that politicians should enter the process only where they added value. In contrast, the Harris government retained the right to make all decisions. The civil servants would recommend to the cabinet, which would then decide. Their view was that since the government was responsible for the outcome, it also had to approve decisions leading to that outcome.

It was apparent to those at the table that the primary goal of CCOP and the representatives of the Privatization Secretariat was the maximization of the sale price of Highway 407. And they were willing to relax various government standards, if this would make the highway more attractive to a prospective purchaser. The career public servants on the committee felt that one of their roles had to be to safeguard the public interest in the face of this overwhelming priority. The policy work was undeniably challenging. Ontario had never before privatized a highway and experience in privatizing existing highways in other jurisdictions was limited. Furthermore, the government's ambitious timetable forced the bureaucracy to work with extraordinary speed to meet deadlines. It was not unusual for staff to be given a stack of documents a foot high to review and comment on in less than 24 hours.

Public servants on the committee did succeed in placing some restrictions and conditions on a prospective concessionaire (Canadian Council for Public-Private Partnerships 2000). These included

- maintaining the land underneath and adjacent to the highway and air rights above it as Crown property,

- regulating Highway 407 as a public highway under the Highway Traffic Act, with the Ontario Provincial Police patrolling it and charging the concessionaire on a full cost-recovery basis,

- applying MTO safety standards and ensuring, through audit and inspection, that such standards are followed,

- ensuring that Highway 407 had the look and feel of a 400-series highway in terms of signage and restrictions on advertising,

- requiring the concessionaire to increase highway capacity if traffic volumes met certain thresholds.

Public servants felt their biggest failure was their inability to persuade the government of the need for a mechanism for regulating tolls. The rate-setting regime described later in this chapter was the most they could prevail on the Harris government to accept.

EVALUATION AND SELECTION

It was the government's view, and the consensus of transportation professionals, that traffic volumes could make Option 1, the extension of the highway to Brock Road in the east, immediately profitable. Its value was estimated by the Finance Ministry as approximately $2.5 billion under a 99-year lease. All other options were expected to cost more to build than they would generate in toll revenues due to insufficient expected traffic volumes. Bids for Options 2, 3 and 4 were therefore anticipated to be considerably lower than for Option 1. Indeed, the Finance Ministry forecasted that completing the highway to Highway 35/115 – i.e. Option 4 - would cost the new owner $1.5 billion (Ibbitson 2000). Finance expected that the biggest cash sale would be for Option 1 and warned that selection of any of the options for the longer highway would be an implicit decision to spend the difference on highway construction, rather than on other priorities.

At the same time, one of the consortia effectively withdrew from the privatization bidding, further narrowing the options. CHIC's financial advisor, Newcourt Credit, was unable to pull the financing together and the incoming Chairman and CEO of the Canadian Imperial Bank of Commerce apparently feared his board would view the project as too risky (Critchley 1999). As a result, CHIC submitted a token bid of a dollar for the privatization, so as to maintain its right to submit a comprehensive bid for the design-build component. Thus there were, in effect, only three bids for the privatization. As had been expected, two of the consortia had their highest bids for Option 1. ORDC's bid was $2.4 billion. 407 International's bid was $2.8 billion. Their bids for Option 4 were over a billion dollars lower, again as expected. To the surprise of the evaluators, Woodbridge not only submitted the highest bid for Option 1 ($2.805 billion), but it also bid an *additional* $25 million for Option 4 – an option which had been estimated to reduce the value of bids significantly.

Selection of the winning bid was to be made by the Cabinet Committee on Privatization, chaired by Finance Minister Ernie Eves. The cabinet as a whole would then ratify the choice. Staff at the Privatization Secretariat kept the CCOP and cabinet in the dark as to the identity of the bidders. Even Carson, the CEO of the Secretariat, was deliberately not informed of this because of his reporting relationship to Minister Sampson. A blind grid was drawn up, showing the bids for each option for each bidder. Bidders were identified only by symbols. When the CCOP met on March 30, it was presented with this grid.

The Woodbridge bid for Option 4 – construction to Highway 35/115 – was the clear favourite. The committee, however, had the right to ask the two top bidders of any option to re-bid if their submissions were within five percent of each other. The Option 1 bids of 407 International and Woodbridge were only $5 million apart, a fraction of a percent. The committee could, therefore, if it chose Option 1 (construction to Brock Road only), create a new auction and possibly obtain a higher price.

The alternatives before the committee were therefore as follows:

1. It could select Option 4 as presented by Woodbridge. For this, the government would receive $2.830 billion. Assuming the environmental assessment process was successfully completed, the entire eastern portion of the highway would be constructed to Highway 35/115. Prior to receiving bids, Ministry of Finance staff had estimated that for such an option the government would receive approximately $1 billion.

2. It could ask Woodbridge and 407 International to bid again under Option 1. This would likely provide an immediate cash benefit to the government in excess of the $2.830 billion under the Option 4 alternative. The eastern terminus of the highway, however, would only be Brock Road in Pickering. For reasons detailed later in this chapter, the remaining portion of the highway would be difficult to construct without a significant cost to the government. The Ministry of Finance had originally estimated that this option (Option 1) would produce approximately $2.5 billion for the government.

The second alternative, asking Woodbridge and 407 International to bid again, would produce the most cash up front for the government, but would delay completion of the entire highway. The first alternative would see the highway completed much sooner than anticipated, and would yield a significantly higher overall return to the government over the longer term. This was because, under the second alternative, the government would have to cover the predicted negative value of the section of highway between Brock Road and Highway 35/115.

At Eves' insistence, the committee chose the second alternative in the expectation that this would provide the greatest immediate cash infusion. Woodbridge and 407 International were asked to re-bid under Option 1. Carson alone carried out this second stage. He contacted the two finalists (he had been made aware of their identities by this time) and asked them to resubmit bids on Option 1 only. 407 International returned with the higher bid of $3.107 billion and was selected. The lease would be for a 99-year period, an unprecedented duration for a toll road concession in the modern era.

The selection of this option can only be explained by the desire of Eves, the Finance Minister, to obtain as much revenue as possible before the election, which would be called on May 5, 1999. He was to present a budget within weeks and was faced with a revenue shortfall. Sources close to the decision-making process within the government have said that there were three priorities – moving towards a balanced budget, cutting taxes, and increasing spending on health care. To do this the government needed the maximum revenue from the sale of Highway 407 and the Option 1 re-bid gave them the means to obtain it.

The government was satisfied with the price that it obtained and had no need to consider its fallback design-build option. This component of the bids was returned unopened to the bidders. Shrewdly, 407 International had not submitted a design – build proposal, significantly minimizing their bidding expenses. They were able to cherry pick from the design work of members of the other, unsuccessful consortia after they won the concession.

CONSEQUENCES

The biggest consequence of not selecting Woodbridge's Option 4 was that construction of the eastern extremity of Highway 407 – the section from Brock Road to Highway 35/115 – would be delayed indefinitely. Had Option 4 been selected, the necessary steps to prepare for construction – route selection, environmental assessment, and property acquisition – would have been initiated. Even though construction itself would be several years away, this section of the highway would have been placed on the fastest track possible. This was the least attractive portion of the highway from a standpoint of traffic volumes and consequential toll collection. Government analysis had come up with a net *cost* of this section as $1.5 billion. Even Woodbridge's bid had assigned a positive value of only $25 million to it, when it was combined with the rest of the highway. As a stand-alone piece of highway, the value would have been much lower.

If the government were to put this section out for tender on its own, it would not be possible to conduct a competition that treated all bidders equally. 407 International, the owner of the existing highway would have several advantages. Other prospective bidders would have the added costs of tying in the tolling system with the rest of Highway 407. An independent highway maintenance system would have to be set up. This would lower the value to bidders of that portion of the franchise. 407 International, alone among potential bidders, would not have to deal with these issues. It would benefit, however, from the construction of Highway 407 East, because the latter would lead to additional trips on the rest of Highway 407 (for example, someone who now drives on

Highway 401 to a cottage in the Kawarthas, but with the extension of Highway 407 to 35/115, shifts to Highway 407). Still, it would not need to bid a high price, because it would be aware of the difficulties facing a competitor's bid. The government was almost certain therefore to receive a lower value for this section of the highway if it were put up for bid on its own. Indeed, it would probably have to pay someone to build and operate it.

Government could, of course, wait until traffic volumes on the eastern part of Highway 407 had grown, so that prospective bidders had greater confidence that the section in question could generate net revenue from tolls. This is not an unrealistic expectation. Forecasts of revenues and traffic volumes on the highway thus far have been understated. It would take time for this traffic growth to develop. In the meantime, the government would have to decide whether it was willing to invest the resources needed for the pre-construction activities described above, something it has not done in the five years since privatization took place.

The most serious consequence of choosing to re-bid Option 1 and maximize pre-election revenues, therefore, is that unless the government is willing to pay for it, the section of 407 from Brock Road to Highway 35/115 will be delayed indefinitely.

THE 99-YEAR LEASE

The 99-year duration of the lease was the most controversial – and surprising – feature of the privatization to outside observers. Participants in the process have described this aspect of the concession as a "travesty." After all, the difference in bid price between a 30-year lease and a 99-year lease was of the order of $100 million on a total price of over $3 billion, depending on the discount rate and toll escalation rates used. The added financial benefit was not particularly significant. In exchange, the government was handing over a lucrative franchise to toll the Highway 407 corridor for almost a century. Leases for highway concessions were generally in the 20 to 30 year range, with a very few in the 50 and 60 year ranges (General Accounting Office 2004). Indeed, some recent leases have been for even shorter, 10 to 15-year terms.

As we have discussed earlier, the Privatization Secretariat and its advisors were able to convince the cabinet that this lease period should be chosen over a shorter one. Given the relatively small financial benefit of entering into the longer term lease, the prime motivator would appear to be ideology; namely, the belief that the private sector was inherently more capable of operating the highway efficiently. They felt that if the government ran it, it would be unable to withstand pressure to veto toll increases, and Highway 407 would end up as congested as Highway 401. Others were less judicious in their remarks, saying that if the highway reverted to the government in 30 years, the government would find a way to "screw it up."

TERMS OF THE CONCESSION

As the successful bidder, 407 International entered into a 99-year lease for the highway corridor, including the existing 69-kilometre long, four to six-lane highway, and associated works such as the tolling equipment and systems. Expansion of the highway from eight to ten lanes was possible. The control centre, call centre and other physical works were also turned over. The tolling and videoimaging technology, however, was the property of Raytheon, which had merged with Hughes in 1997.

The consortium was allowed to develop the corridor for highway related purposes only. For example, it could build a patrol yard, but not a shopping mall. Rights to other uses of the corridor, such as telecommunication lines, remained with the government.

407 International also incurred the obligation to complete the deferred interchanges on the existing highway, as well as to build the 24-kilometre western extension, and the 15-kilometre eastern extension to Brock Road (see map on page 70). The western extension opened on July 18, 2001 and the eastern extension on August 30, 2001. The previously constructed, but closed, section from McCowan Road to Markham Road was opened on June 24, 1999, a month after 407 International assumed control of the highway. They did not have to concern themselves with the discharging of large volumes of traffic onto Markham Road in the way that the OTCC, a Crown corporation, did. It remained the eastern terminus for two years until the eastern extension was completed.

407 International was permitted to toll all sections of the highway. There were sections in the concession agreement that dealt with congestion, toll rates, and lane expansion. These are described more fully later in this chapter. Penalties for non-payment of tolls and other fees or penalties would be enforced by MTO, which would deny licence plate registrations to defaulters. There was an escalating limit on permissi-

ble administration fees. The setting of all other fees, penalties and interest rates was left up to the concessionaire. Customer service levels, such as wait times to answer telephones at the call centre, were also not specified.

The Ontario Provincial Police would provide policing services on the corridor. Their fee schedule was based on the full cost of providing these services. This was primarily intended to be for traffic safety purposes, but enforcement was also carried out against people who attempted to evade toll payment, for example by obscuring licence plates.

COMPLETING THE PRIVATIZATION

The government was anxious to conclude the privatization deal because of its electoral schedule. The share purchase agreement was signed on April 12, 1999 and negotiations to finalize the contract proceeded rapidly. A provincial budget was delivered on May 4. Net proceeds of $1.6 billion from the sale of Highway 407 – the sale price of $3.1 billion less the $1.5 billion book value of the highway – were included in revenue for the 1999-2000 fiscal year. Helped by this revenue, the budget projected a deficit of $2.1 billion, which was $500 million better than the deficit target previously set out in the balanced budget plan (Hansard 1999).[3] The budget featured additional spending on healthcare, as well as a tax rebate of $200 for every taxpayer. The 407 deal was to have closed on May 3, but was delayed. It closed on May 5, the day the provincial election was called.

REACTION

The government's spin on the privatization was that it had sold a highway that had cost $1.5 billion to build for $3.1 billion and had made a "profit" of $1.6 billion. It portrayed the requirement that the concessionaire build east and west extensions as saving the government $800 million. In the words of Minister Sampson, "All of this is at no additional cost to the taxpayer. Nobody is going to be coming to us in 30 years saying this bridge is falling down, you need to put $20 million in to redo a bridge. These are sizeable costs that we have pushed off to the private sector" (Crone 1999). As we explain later in this chapter, this misrepresented the nature of the sale.

There were dissenting voices. The Canadian Automobile Association pointed out that the tolls would now be charged for 99 years, compared with the previous estimate of 30 years or less (Girard 1999). *The Toronto Star*, in pre-election mode on behalf of the opposition Liberals, wrote a scathing editorial titled "Tolls forever" (Toronto Star 1999). It described the sale as a "rotten deal for the travelers who use the highway" and "selling someone [the consortium] the right to hold people to ransom." The editorial added that travelers who used Highway 407 would "no longer just be paying for the cost of the road, which is what they were promised when it was built. They will now be paying for the $1.6 billion profit the province has already made as well as any extra profits the consortium can make by jacking up tolls." The criticism was not sustained, however. The impression that seemed to stay with the public was that the government had made "a good deal," doubling the original investment.

TURNOVER OF THE HIGHWAY

The turnover of the highway to 407 International was carried out smoothly. The formal transaction consisted of the acquisition of the shares of the newly named 407 ETR Concession Company. 407 International took over the offices and assets of the OTCC. They initially retained the services of CHMC to operate Highway 407, gradually replacing it with their own operation.

OTCC staff had cleanup duties before the handover. Confidential material such as cabinet documents and government personnel files were removed. Some of the OTCC staff, such as David Garner, retired from the OPS. Others who were permanent members of the OPS returned to their original departments. Contract staff simply had their contracts terminated. A few staff who returned to MTO were told they had to accept demotions upon their return because they had received unwarranted promotions at the OTCC. They tended to view this as indicative of resentment within MTO for their association with the OTCC. They were returning, however, to a much smaller and differently structured ministry with far fewer available positions than when they had left it, so their view is open to some debate.

THE ROYAL BANK'S ROLE

The Royal Bank of Canada had played a role in each step of the privatization process. RBC Capital Markets had advised the Privatization Secretariat as to whether Highway 407 should be privatized and whether the privatization should take the form of an IPO or outright sale. Its recommendation was to sell Highway 407. Fortuitously for RBC, it was the choice that would continue to give it the greatest financial benefit, because it remained an adviser on the privatization itself, with the amount of compensation tied to the revenues received by the government.

RBC Capital Markets' advice on critical issues, such as the duration of the lease, was consistently in the direction of maximizing the immediate return to government. As discussed earlier, it coincidentally provided the greatest immediate cash influx at the expense of the long-term public interest. In fairness, however, it must be acknowledged that its opinions were generally shared within the Privatization Secretariat and the decision not to complete the highway in the east was pushed by the Minister of Finance.

RBC Dominion Securities was also a part of the financial consortium that backed 407 International's bid. As such, it benefited from the advice that its sister organization was giving the Privatization Secretariat. Furthermore, the Royal Bank was a lender to both the Woodbridge and 407 International consortia and stood to benefit if either were awarded the concession. It had received clearance for this role from the government three weeks before the bids were to be submitted, in recognition that several lenders would be required to handle the size of the debt.

Several people close to the bidding process have expressed discomfort at what they perceived as a conflict of interest. Standard practice in such situations is for the financial institution to erect a "Chinese wall" ensuring that there is no communication of information between the different parts. RBC gave specific written undertakings to the Secretariat that such a boundary was in place. The leadership of the Privatization Secretariat knew the people involved at RBC. This apparently contributed to their faith that RBC would honour this undertaking. As to the Royal Bank's role as lender, when the bids were submitted, guaranteed financing for each bid had to be locked in. This meant that $10 to $12 billion was tied up in the banking system. The magnitude of the financing required made it virtually impossible to exclude Canada's largest financial institution and still have the necessary pool of capital available.

VALUE OF THE HIGHWAY

When the Harris government sold Highway 407 in 1999 for $3.1 billion, it hailed the deal as a signal success, yielding a "profit" of $1.6 billion over its original cost. Just over two and a half years later, SNC Lavalin sold a part of its holding to Grupo Ferrovial at a price that established the value of the highway at $6.3 billion, twice the price at which it was sold in 1999 by the government (Smith 2002).[4] The opposition seized on this to attack the government, claiming this indicated that the price paid in 1999 was too low. Yet the 1999 sale was by a competitive bidding process and could reasonably be said to have established the market price at that time. Why then this doubling of price in such a short time?[5]

To answer, we must compare the highway in 2002 and at the time of sale in 1999. In 2002, there were 39 additional kilometres, constructed at an additional cost of approximately $507 million (407 International 2004). Hence, merely calculating by the sale price, the value of the highway could be expected to rise to $3.6 billion, still $2.7 billion less than the market value barely two years later. Standard and Poor valued the highway in late 2003 at between $8 and $13 billion (Globe and Mail 2003). The upper limit would give an astounding difference of 260%.

Once again, it is important to look at what was actually sold in 1999. This was not merely an assembly of capital works. The primary sale was of the concession to toll, with an obligation to maintain the corridor for a period of 99 years. The value of this concession was determined by the anticipated future stream of revenues, which in turn was a function of the volume of traffic and the level of tolls that could be charged.

In 1999, the completed central portion of the highway had been in operation for less than two years and traffic was still growing. The average trip on the 69-kilometre central portion of the highway was 9 kilometres. When the 24-kilometre western extension was completed after the sale, the average trip on the highway was 19 kilometres. Not only were average daily traffic volumes growing, the trips were longer, compounding the increase in revenues.

In 1999, tolls were being set by the OTCC at levels its market analysis determined to be maximizing revenue and that would also recover costs and pay off the debt over a 30-year period. By 2002, the new owner was able to raise tolls well beyond the threshold prescribed in the concession agreement and continue to see traffic volumes grow. The highway was proving to be even more profitable than had been forecast in 1999.

Why then was this not reflected in the purchase bids? The simple answer is that the private sector was notoriously risk averse. Given less than two years of operation, it was not willing to place a higher value on the concession. (Recall the bids in 1993, where loan guarantees were requested for what turned out to be a very profitable venture, or CIBC's withdrawal from CHIC's privatization bid.) By 2002, however, there was sufficient operating experience to demonstrate that the risks were negligible, while the potential profits were enormous.

When it sold the highway in 1999, therefore, the Harris government almost certainly received the highest price from the private sector it could have obtained at that time. But by selling it when it did, with operating experience so limited, it probably obtained a much lower price than it could have had it waited a few years. At the very least, it is unlikely that it would have done any worse. Once again, the desperation to raise money before an election resulted in a failure to serve the public's best interest.

Anthony Fell, Chairman of RBC Capital Markets, spoke about the Highway 407 privatization to a conference on public private partnerships (Fell 2002). The speech is fascinating both for what was said and what wasn't. He considered the privatization a major success and strongly defended the doubling of the highway's value in private hands, likening it to the doubling or tripling in value that some companies have experienced after an IPO. The analogy is inappropriate, because there was no IPO and because it was OTCC, not 407 International, that developed the highway. Had the government delayed the privatization or, as will be discussed in more detail in chapter 9, retained a stake in the highway after privatization in 1999, it could have claimed more of that increase in value for the public interest. Fell also repeated the claim that in 1999 the Ontario government had made twice what it had cost to build the highway – a misleading statement, as we have previously noted. If he in fact believed this, it calls into question RBC Capital Markets' understanding of precisely what it was advising on. What Fell did not mention was the roles of RBC Capital Markets and RBC Dominion Securities in the privatization. Just as investment advisers who write about particular companies are expected to declare their holdings in those companies, we think that investment bankers who offer advice about public policy ought to declare their own interests.

RISING TOLLS, GROWING CONTROVERSY

The sale of the highway raised concerns and criticism from a variety of sources. The main criticism was that tolls were bound to increase when the private sector took over the highway. The government attempted to counter this. The Office of Privatization, successor to the Privatization Secretariat, issued a background document claiming that toll increases would be at the rate of inflation plus two percent until 2014, and at the inflation rate thereafter. Indeed, the release claimed that utilizing this formula, over the first 15 years tolls could only increase by about 3 cents per kilometre (Office of Privatization 1999). Rob Sampson, the Minister for Privatization, reassured the public that "tolls would not skyrocket because new owners need drivers if they are to pay off debts. The limit is what the market is prepared to pay and that's a realistic limit" (Lindgren 1999). Other ministers made similar statements. Sampson did not remind people of his previous remarks that tolls, if anything, would drop.

Public servants who were familiar with the provisions of the contract governing toll rates were aghast at these statements. As users soon realized, the comments were, at the very least, misleading. 407 International raised off-peak toll rates in September 1999 by approximately 12%. In less than four years, toll rates had risen by 29.5% in peak hours and 73% in off-peak hours. Furthermore, the peak period was expanded by an hour. A section of the concession contract, the "Tolling, Congestion Relief and Expansion Agreement," spells out the restrictions on toll rates. It is summarized in the next section. All toll increases have been entirely in compliance with the agreement. The most charitable explanation for Sampson's and other ministers' statements about toll rates was they did not understand the agreement they had approved.

TOLLING, CONGESTION RELIEF, AND EXPANSION

As noted above, a section of the concession contract describes the restrictions on toll rates. It also describes the requirements for lane expansion. The rationale for this agreement is to ensure that traffic continues to use Highway 407 and thus relieve congestion on other highways.

The agreement itself is complex and encompasses several types of vehicles and scenarios. We have not attempted to restate it here. What follows is a generalized description that should provide the reader with a reasonable understanding of how it works.

Two parameters, the "toll threshold" and "traffic threshold" are used to determine appropriate toll levels. We start at a base year. The traffic level is defined at 95% of actual volume in this base year. Traffic volume is measured in vehicles per lane. A predicted or target rate of growth, from one to three percent, is used to set target traffic flow for each year. Growth is not expected to be linear, but to gradually slow down, as lanes fill up. This is factored into the model and a traffic threshold growth index is generated for each year. This index is applied to the base traffic level. The result is the "traffic threshold" for a given year. This quantity is dependent only on actual traffic volumes in the base year and on the growth index, which is a mathematical expression. It does not incorporate any other measured results.

A similar method is used to generate a standard value for toll rates. Starting with an initial "toll threshold" of 11 cents per kilometre, an escalation factor of the consumer price index plus two percent is applied to produce a "toll threshold" for each succeeding year. The "toll threshold" serves as a lower limit for toll rates and should not be exceeded if traffic volume does not reach the traffic threshold. Penalties are assessed if this restriction is violated. As long as traffic volume does not fall below the traffic threshold, however, there is no restriction whatsoever on the ability of the concessionaire to raise tolls.

Given the rapid growth of development around the Highway 407 corridor, traffic levels seem set to continue an almost unabated growth, with little danger of falling below the threshold. Tolls are therefore likely to continue to increase beyond the threshold level. As David Turnbull, the then minister of transportation remarked, when 407 International raised toll rates for the second time, effective May 2000, "The people of Ontario who are using the highway are voting with their wheels." He was then reported as adding that if motorists did not like using Highway 407, they should stop using it and battle congestion on Highway 401 or other public roads (Brennan 2000b). At each toll rate increase, ministers would essentially repeat the same message; namely, that market forces were regulating the toll rates, and that if motorists did not like the tolls, they should stop using Highway 407. Of course, the government had no power to intervene even if it wanted to. 407 International was adhering to its agreements, as far as setting toll rates was concerned. That, at least, was the interpretation of the Harris and Eves governments. The McGuinty government appears to have a different viewpoint, which we discuss later.

The agreement also states that if traffic exceeds 1700 vehicles in a lane for 125 hours in a calendar year, 407 International must add a lane in that segment of the highway. This has been done in a section of the highway in Mississauga. Ironically, the concessionaire cited this as a reason why tolls had to increase once again, though the toll regulating formula was not affected by this additional capacity.

There is a provision within the agreement that after five years, the two parties can negotiate an amendment to it at the request of one of the parties. The purpose of such an amendment would be to realize more fully the intent of the original agreement. It may not materially change the current or future earnings of the concessionaire. We will return to this point in the context of the McGuinty government's attempt to control the setting of toll rates.

FEES, PENALTIES, AND CUSTOMER SERVICE

When 407 International took over the highway, it raised the various administration fees. Penalties for late payments were also doubled from $15 to $30. As provided for in the contract, MTO denied vehicle registrations to owners who were in default.

Barring use of a vehicle for non-payment of a civil debt has been a further source of contention. The rationale, however, is easy to follow. Highway 407 is an open access electronic toll highway. Unlike most toll highways, use is not limited to vehicles equipped with transponders (trucks and trailers are required to use transponders), nor are tolls manually collected at physical barriers. Any driver can use the highway. If they are not equipped with transponders, they are invoiced after the fact. The typical toll on Highway 407 for a private vehicle is approximately $3. It is easy to see that for most casual or infrequent users of the highway, non-payment of tolls could be a sound business decision. They would be challenging the concessionaire to spend much more on collection than the value of the debt itself. There would also be less incentive for motorists to use transponders, which is, in essence, prepayment of tolls. Leakage of revenues could be significant. Paradoxically, therefore, the smaller the debt, the more important it becomes to invoke a sanction that is a sufficiently strong deterrent. This is the reasoning behind plate denial for non-payment of parking tickets, a seemingly trivial offence in the minds of most drivers. Invoking it for non-payment of tolls is similar.

Some critics argued that while the government may use this sanction, it should not be available to a private operator of the highway. Clearly, though, the ability of the operator to receive revenues is a key determinant in valuing the highway. Absent such a sanction, the value of the highway would be much lower and the lease price would have been lower.

Given the severity of the sanction, care must be taken to ensure that when it is applied, it is done with deliberation and without error. A multi-stage process for licence plate denial was therefore designed and spelled out in regulations. A driver who was 90 days in default would have to be notified by registered mail that unless her account was settled, her vehicle registration would not be renewed when it expired. If the account remained delinquent, a second letter would be sent, also by registered mail, stating that MTO had been instructed not to renew the vehicle registration. Receipt of these registered letters had to be verified by signature to ensure that the driver had been properly notified. At that point, MTO would also receive a notification to that effect from 407 International.

In practice, the concessionaire was not following this process. Formal notifications were not being sent by registered mail. 407 International was simply informing the Registrar of Motor Vehicles, an MTO official, of the licence plates that should not be renewed. Drivers who did not receive these letters, because they had moved, for instance, would appear at an MTO office to renew their vehicle registrations and be refused. An additional problem was that some of these people claimed that they had paid their invoices. Others denied that they had used the highway. When they tried to contact 407 International by phone, they were placed on hold for interminable lengths of time and were unable to have their disputes resolved. In the meantime, MTO was not allowing them to renew their licence plates.

While aware of this growing problem, the Harris government initially chose not to act. It felt that acknowledging the issue would be a tacit admission of problems with the privatization. When these unfortunate drivers' tales of woe were reported to the media (Barber 2000a, 2000b), the government was forced to respond. After acknowledging that "thousands of motorists" had been unable to renew their vehicle registrations, Premier Harris said that he had asked for a report on the matter (Mackie 2000). The government was dealing with growing anger in the politically important 905 belt of the GTA (so called for its geographic location outside Metro Toronto's 416 area code), as 80,000 motorists had already been faced with plate denial when attempting to renew their licences. An additional 110,000 motorists had been reported to MTO as having delinquent accounts. Under the policy in place, MTO would have to deny them licence plate renewal as well (Mallan 2000).

On February 21, 2000, John Ibbitson's (2000) story about the 407 privatization process appeared and once again put the government on the defensive. Two days later, on February 23, Premier Harris described the vehicle registration situation as a "screw-up" and "not acceptable" (Brennan 2000a). Taking his cue, Transportation Minister Turnbull announced the next day that withholding plate renewals had been "suspended until such a time as [407 International] have completely implemented all the ways to completely resolve these matters." Jose Maria Lopez de Fuentes, the President and CEO of 407 International, acknowledged the problems and promised to resolve them. As a start, the number of telephone operators at their call centre would be doubled. He anticipated that the problem would be cleared in four to eight weeks (Mallan 2000).

In mid-2000, apparently preparing to reinstate the suspension of plate renewals, the government quietly changed the regulations so that registered notifications to delinquent account holders were no longer required. In effect, this regularized 407 International's previous practices. It also had the effect of reducing the cost of the plate denial process to the concessionaire. Yet, the government would appear to have had second thoughts. Four years have elapsed and the sanction of licence plate suspension has not been reinstated. Despite the efforts of the concessionaire to improve customer service and resolve billing disputes, it is, in the government's view, still unable to generate a completely error-free list of delinquent accounts. Interestingly, though, the Highway 407 website (www.407etr.com) states that it "may send outstanding accounts to the Registrar of Motor Vehicles for plate denial," strongly implying that plate denial has been restored as a sanction. Apparently the ambiguous "may" was substituted for the more definitive "will" at the government's insistence.

Late payment fees constituted a further problem for 407 International. On assuming control of the highway, it had raised the fee for payments over 90 days in arrears from $15 to $30. A class action had been launched on behalf of approximately 840,000 drivers who had been subject to this fee, on the grounds that the fee was unenforceable and that it unjustly enriched the company. In April 2003, the action was settled. 407 International agreed to give a $6 credit to all those who had paid this fee. It also agreed to refund the entire late payment fee of $30, if it could be shown that it should not have been charged. The late payment fee was reduced to $12.50 for accounts that were over three months in arrears. An additional fee of $12.50 was added to accounts that were sent out for collection (Perkins 2003). In the absence of plate denial, this is the only way in which 407 International can seek payment from delinquent accounts.

THE MCGUINTY GOVERNMENT

Toll levels on Highway 407 were an issue during the 2003 Ontario election, especially in the critical "905" belt of suburban ridings that ring Toronto. The Liberals, led by Dalton McGuinty, pledged to force rollbacks of toll levels if they were elected.[6] When they took office in October 2003, they began scrutinizing the contract to determine how they could fulfill this pledge. Initial media reports suggested that they would be unable to find any room to manoeuvre (Lindgren 2003, Globe and Mail 2003). The bond rating agencies also offered the (unsolicited) advice that the contract was ironclad.

To further exacerbate the government's discomfort, 407 International announced that on February 1, 2004 it would increase tolls by one cent per kilometre for cars, two cents per kilometre for light trucks, and three cents per kilometre for heavy trucks, during both peak and off-peak periods.

Because of the $5 billion deficit it inherited, the McGuinty government had been forced to backtrack on many of its election promises. It appeared, however, determined to maintain its political credibility in this instance at least. It claimed that tolls could not be raised without its permission. Furthermore, if 407 International proceeded on this course, it would be in breach of contract. The clause in the agreement that it cited states that the concessionaire must obtain the government's permission before making any material changes to the highway. The Harris and Eves governments had only applied this provision to physical activities, such as construction. The concessionaire disputed the McGuinty government's expanded interpretation of this clause and it proceeded with the announced rate increase as scheduled.

Claiming that 407 International's actions effectively voided the contract, the government went to the Ontario Superior Court to seek such a ruling (Ministry of Transportation 2004a). The court, however, directed it to first utilize the dispute resolution mechanism provided for in the contract. To the government's dismay, the arbitrator ruled that changing toll levels did not constitute a material change to the highway and that 407 International did not require the government's permission to do so. Transportation Minister Harinder Takhar issued a statement that he would appeal the ruling. In his view, it was "inconceivable that any government would have given a private consortium the unfettered right to raise tolls for 99 years" (Babbage 2004). Of course, in the arbitrator's view, the Harris government had apparently done the inconceivable.

Users of the highway appear to be squarely on the side of the government. Put simply, they would like lower tolls, though they apparently have not made the connection between the absence of congestion and toll levels. On the other side, backing the concessionaire's right to set its toll levels are the less numerous but influential bond rating agencies and business organizations, as well as some sections of the media (Globe and Mail 2004), warning the government of the consequences for investor confidence if what they view as a straightforward commercial contract is the subject of endless litigation.

The government also reiterated its intention to renegotiate the contract. This could have taken place as early as April 2004, five years after the initial signing, but the preceding actions had rendered this moot, for the time being at least. According to the minister, the renegotiation clause was there to permit the parties "to assess whether the arrangement is achieving the purposes of the agreement and serving the public interest." The reference to public interest appears to have been the minister's own construction, as it is not explicitly mentioned in the relevant section of the agreement. What is specifically protected from the government's standpoint are its objectives in the areas of congestion relief, open access, truck access and lane expansion (Concession agreement, Schedule 22, Section 6.1). Furthermore, lowering tolls would, of course, reduce the concessionaire's earnings, a consequence that is also specifically prohibited in the renegotiation clause. Presumably, the government's strategy as it pursues this approach will become more apparent with time.

Yet another area of dispute had risen between the government and 407 International. Under the agreement, the company was required to provide the province with annual audited traffic reports. As described previously in this chapter, traffic volumes determine whether the concessionaire must pay penalties, or whether lanes must be added. These reports are therefore vitally important to both parties. The Government disputed the numbers provided to them for 2001 and 2002, despite the fact that they were certified by external, independent auditors (Arthur

Andersen and Deloitte & Touche respectively). In 2003, the company and the province agreed that if a second independent auditor did not identify any material issues, this opinion would be final and binding on both parties. The independent audits were performed by BDO Dunwoody and resulted in unqualified opinions. The province, however, refused to accept this audit either. 407 International has filed a judicial application to enforce this agreement.

Prior to the eruption of this recent controversy, there had been a general perception that plate denial had been restored. Certainly, 407 International's website supported that impression. Currently, there are 600,000 transponders in circulation, and transponder usage accounts for 78 % of daily trips on the highway (407 International 2004). 407 International reports a total of $15 million in unpaid tolls. Ontarians are generally regarded as law-abiding. However, there are apparently about 8000 drivers who have accumulated unpaid tolls of $1000 to $5000 and refuse to pay. Without the sanction of plate denial, the concessionaire must use less efficient methods, such as small claims court and collection agencies to pursue these debtors. (Willis 2004). It will be interesting to observe whether transponder usage declines and unpaid tolls increase as the controversy receives further publicity and drivers realize that the remedies for the concessionaire are more limited. Clearly, it is to the company's advantage to have the sanction of plate denial restored as soon as possible. In July 2004, it sued the government to compel it to implement the provision in the contract which denied licence plate renewals to users of the highway who had unpaid toll bills (Mackie 2004b). Transportation Minister Takhar responded that since the billing problems had not been resolved to the government's satisfaction, the sanction would not be restored. He claimed that earlier in the year when the province had attempted to send in an auditor to check the concessionaire's systems related to plate denial, he had been turned away. The minister went on to say that the decision was up to the Registrar of Motor Vehicles, who was responsible for licensing motor vehicles. While the Minister described the registrar as an independent, quasi-judicial provincial official, the holder of that title is also the Assistant Deputy Minister of Road User Safety, an official within the department (Ministry of Transportation 2004b).

The government opened yet another front in its war with 407 International by challenging its use of 2002, rather than an earlier year, as the "base year" when setting the toll formulas described previously in this chapter. If upheld, this would result in 407 International incurring severe financial penalties because it did not add capacity soon enough (Ministry of Transportation 2004c).

The dispute then took on an international flavour. The Spanish government reportedly threatened to scuttle a proposed Trade and Investment Enhancement Agreement between Canada and the European Union unless Ontario backed down in its confrontation with 407 International. The rationale for Spain's interest is that 407 International is ostensibly Spanish-controlled. In actual fact, the indirect controlling interest in 407 International is Australian, as described earlier in this chapter. Premier McGuinty responded that Ontario had the responsibility to, as he put it, "protect the interests of its citizens" (Ibbitson 2004). These disputes demonstrate the increasingly acrimonious relationship that has developed between the provincial government and 407 International. The McGuinty government, as we have noted earlier, seems determined to maintain some political credibility by at least curbing the right of the concessionaire to raise tolls. 407 International, on the other hand, takes the position that it has a valid contract with the government. It intends to protect the legal and contractual rights that it believes flow from this. The bond rating agencies have also expressed their concerns. They have pointed out that a number of areas of the highway's operations are dependent on cooperation between the government and the concessionaire. Consequently, the current state of the relationship could affect 407 International's ability to refinance its bonds (Willis 2004). The government may therefore still have leverage with 407 International in this area, though it states that there is no linkage between plate denial and the issues of contract renegotiation or toll rates.

We await the outcome of this conflict.

CONCLUSIONS

In discussing the privatization, it is important to draw a distinction between the actual process that was followed and the policy decisions that were made. The Privatization Secretariat crafted a relatively sound process, designed to open the bidding to as many qualified consortia as possible. Necessary expertise was drawn from within the government and externally. A decision-making structure for obtaining direction on policy and ultimately for selecting the successful bidder and bid option was created and adhered to. The usefulness of certain aspects of the process, such as the indicative bid step, may be debated, but these cannot be described as fundamental flaws.

If, however, the prohibitions of the bid document which prohibited contact between members of the consortia and the cabinet were disregarded by key decision makers in the Harris government, as has been claimed, the integrity of the process was compromised. We do not know whether this affected the policy decisions that were made. Nonetheless, the decisions described below must give an observer pause.

A private sector owner of the highway must borrow at a higher cost than the government. A profit must also be generated. As a consequence, users of the privatized 407 would have been expected to pay more than when the highway was owned by the government. This in itself may be considered a drawback of privatizing the highway.

The issue of privatization extends beyond the economic into the philosophical and political realms. The decision makers in the Harris government and their advisors had an ideological aversion to government operation of the highway. They believed that the private sector would necessarily operate the highway more efficiently than a government entity. Perhaps this is what led Ministers Sampson and Clement to make the implausible assertion that toll rates would actually come down when they announced the impending privatization of the highway.

It is evident that many elements of the privatization were antithetical to the long-term public interest. The timing of the privatization was dictated by the government's political and electoral needs and was undoubtedly premature. By not waiting till the highway had been operational for a longer period, and more actual operating data had been obtained, the government did not sufficiently minimize the risk factor for private sector investors. This resulted in a much lower price than would have been realized had they waited a few more years and observed the steady growth in traffic. The Harris government did receive the revenues it needed for its pre-election spending and was able to satisfy its supporters that it was indeed committed to privatization, but it probably sacrificed several billion dollars to do so.

The toll increases since privatization have been discussed in some detail earlier in this chapter. Clearly, the toll rate provisions in the contract are advantageous to the concessionaire, particularly as development in the regions surrounding the corridor grows. The government was trying to increase the value of the highway for a sale or long-term lease. There is little dispute that Highway 407 is functioning smoothly and doing its job of helping to ease congestion in the GTA. Our criticism is that the citing of pure market theory by the Harris government as justification for toll rate increases ignores the fact that Highway 407 has become a highway of necessity for many users living in the 905 belt. 407 International has been provided with a captive market.

The 99-year period of the lease is unprecedented in the history of modern concession agreements for toll highways. For a premium of the order of $100 million on a $3 billion bid, the Harris government ensured that the great-great-grandchildren of current users will continue to pay tolls on the corridor.

The selection of the option that took the eastern terminus of highway only to Brock Road, rather than to Highway 35/115, gave an immediate revenue premium of $300 million. The consequence of this action is much more expensive in the longer term. The completion of the highway will undoubtedly be delayed. The Harris government's then finance minister, Jim Flaherty, who was an MPP for the area, announced in May 2001 that the government would call for proposals to build 407 East to 35/115 (Toronto Star 2001). Flaherty did not mention a time line. As noted earlier, there is a vast amount of preparatory work to be done before construction can begin. The call for proposals had still not gone out up to the time that the government was defeated two and a half years later. When this section is built, 407 International will have a significant advantage in any new competition, as we have discussed earlier, with a further discounting of the bids as a result.

The arrival of the McGuinty government, with an election promise to roll back toll rates, and its subsequent confrontation with 407 International has opened a new chapter in the highway's saga. It is evident that this government does not subscribe to the laissez-faire views of the Harris and Eves governments. Its hands may have been tied, however, by its predecessors' actions. At the time of writing, it is unclear how this will be resolved.

Finally, consider some of the Rae government's longer-term objectives when Highway 407 was being planned as a toll highway. Congestion was to be eased; the highway was to be a showcase for the Ontario engineering and road building industries; and tolls were to end when the original investment was paid for, and the highway would revert to the provincial highway system. Congestion has certainly been eased, but the Harris government's legacy is a highway owned and operated by Australian, Spanish and Québec firms, with minimal Ontario content. Tolls will now stay on for 99 years, many decades after the highway has been paid for.

CHAPTER 9

EVALUATION AND CONCLUSION

Previous chapters have told the story of Highway 407 as a major transportation infrastructure project, involving complex and ongoing
relationships between the public and private sectors. We examined the
initiation of the project, the process of contracting with two private sector consortia, the management of the project by a special purpose
Crown corporation, and the subsequent privatization of the highway.
This chapter concludes our study by evaluating Highway 407 from the
following perspectives:

1. Highway 407 as a large project with a critical information
   technology component
2. the role of political and bureaucratic leadership
3. OTCC as a management structure for a large project
4. the fairness of the bidding process for the initial contracts and
   subsequent privatization, and the transparency of the process, in
   terms of whether the public has the right to know about the
   entirety of these contracts
5. the appropriateness of the level of tolls on Highway 407
6. alternatives to the privatization contract signed by the
   Harris government.

This wide range of issues reflects the complexity of the project and the
range of important spheres of public sector activity that it has involved.
These are also evaluative issues and this chapter represents our judg-
ments upon them. Many remain unresolved and open to public debate.
We expect, therefore, that Highway 407 will remain a topic of political
interest and possible regulation and that road pricing will remain an
issue of political controversy in the greater Toronto area and elsewhere
for some time to come. A clear account of Highway 407's history can
inform future discussion, and we draw several conclusions regarding
transportation policy and public administration that we hope will contribute to the continuing debate.

HIGHWAY 407 AS A LARGE IT-BASED PROJECT

While over 90% of the cost of Highway 407 was for roadworks, the remaining 10% spent on tolling was essential to transforming an ordinary highway into a smart highway that would be able to recover its costs automatically. From this standpoint, we consider Highway 407 as an IT-based project. There is substantial international experience, in both the public and private sectors, that managing large IT-based projects is always challenging, and that such projects are prone either to outright failure or at least disappointment in delivering less than promised. The Standish Group (www.standishgroup.com), an IT consultancy, has made a lucrative business of tracking the performance of large IT projects and suggesting improvements. Using their definition of a successful project as one that is completed within budget, on time, and with full functionality, the group's initial 1995 study of 8400 projects in the public and private sectors in the US found that only 16% were successful, 31% were cancelled, and 53% were compromised (late, over budget, or delivered less than full functionality). The group's subsequent study of IT projects in the US in 2000 found that the situation had improved somewhat, as 28% were successful, 23 % were cancelled, and 49% were compromised. Their 2003 report found additional improvement, with 33 percent successful, 17% cancelled, and 50% compromised (www.standishgroup.com).

The Organisation for Economic Co-operation and Development (OECD) held an expert meeting on managing large public sector IT projects in October 2000, hearing reports from eleven national governments, including Canada, the US, and the UK. The meeting concluded that project management problems on a scale and of a frequency identified by the Standish Group pose a major challenge to implementing e-government plans and suggested ways to deal with these problems (OECD 2001). More recently, the UK Parliamentary Office of Science and Technology (2003) reviewed that country's experience managing large public sector projects and produced its own best practice suggestions.

Why are large IT-based projects so problematic? For deeper insight, we turn to the analytic framework developed by Globerman and Vining (1996). They identified three main environmental factors that affect procurement decisions: task complexity, contestability, and asset specificity. Task complexity describes the degree of difficulty in specifying and monitoring the conditions of a transaction. Contestability refers to the number of firms currently or potentially available to bid for a government contract. Asset specificity denotes the extent to which an asset makes a necessary contribution to the production of a particular good only, with a much lower value in alternative uses. Two polar cases in this framework are low complexity, high contestability, and low asset specificity, on the one hand, and high complexity, low contestability, and high asset specificity, on the other. The former is the most favourable case for a government that is contracting out. Low complexity implies that the government can readily specify and monitor the contract, high contestability means that there are many actual or potential bidders, and low asset specificity means that assets produced for the project can be redeployed readily elsewhere. From the government's point of view, this situation means that inefficient or opportunistic contractors can quickly be replaced; from the contractor's point of view it means that opportunism on the part of the government is not a concern, because the product can be sold to someone else.

A mixture of high task complexity, low contestability, and high asset specificity is the most difficult case for both government and contractor. It is also the case represented by many large IT projects. The government will have difficulty specifying and monitoring outcomes because the contractor's work is inherently complicated (for example, writing tolling system software involving millions of lines of code). Low contestability means that there are few actual or potential bidders; in the case of Highway 407, there were only two consortia. Asset specificity means that bidders are concerned about the possibility of opportunism on the part of government because the assets they produce, for example software specific to a government program, will be less valuable to anyone else. High asset specificity was less applicable to Highway 407 because a tolling system integrating videoimaging and transponders and linked to a vehicle registration database would, with some changes, be applicable elsewhere. This would reduce the contractor's fear of exploitation by the Ontario government.

If large IT-based projects are so problematic, why does the public sector undertake so many of them? Often there is no choice. In many instances (for example, air traffic control) legacy systems using outdated software operating on mainframe computers have reached the end of their useful life and must be replaced. Similarly, as discussed in chapter 2, the Ontario government faced a traffic congestion problem in the greater Toronto area that could not be ignored. As discussed in chapter 3, because of the deficits of the early Nineties, the government could not find funding for it in the operating budget, necessitating tolling to produce a revenue stream to cover the highway. The tolling had to be electronic because of the impracticality of using toll booths on an urban expressway. MTO lacked the technical expertise to build an electronic toll road itself, thus requiring it to be contracted out.

By the Standish Group's criteria, Highway 407 was a compromised project. While it had full functionality, it was over budget and late. In terms of cost, the road itself was within its budget of $930 million, and CHIC earned a $6 million bonus for early completion. Safety modifications recommended by the Professional Engineers of Ontario's expert committee and accepted by Minister Palladini added $15 million to the construction cost. The tolling technology ultimately cost approximately $90 million, which was at least $13 million over budget.[1] The $13 million overrun was due to OTCC's decision to double videoimaging capacity. The consortium incurred additional costs to fulfill its obligation to complete the project, but, except for the $1 million it paid in penalties to OTCC, these were not disclosed. In terms of delay, Highway 407 was to be in operation with tolls being collected from drivers with transponders on December 31, 1996 and from drivers without transponders on March 31, 1997. As discussed in chapter 7, the highway opened without tolls on June 7, 1997 and the complete tolling technology was operational on October 14, 1997. A measure of the cost of delay is lost revenue. At the outset the highway was producing revenues of $5 million per month, so that a delay of almost 10 months in tolling resulted in lost revenues of approximately $50 million. In total, adding the $15 million in extra cost due to safety modifications, $13 million cost overrun for tolling technology, and $50 million for lost revenue due to lateness, Highway 407 cost at least $80 million more than originally budgeted. The government assessed the total cost of the highway at $1.5 billion. The relevant question is the significance of a cost overrun of $80 million relative to a budget of $1.5 billion. As a proportion of total cost, 5 percent is not large.

Another way to evaluate the performance of Highway 407 as a technology and construction project is in terms of its net present value. An evaluation of this nature occurred when the highway was privatized in 1999 and the government received $3.1 billion. The winning consortium accepted the obligation to build another 39 kilometres of the highway, and was entitled to collect tolls on all 108 kilometres of the completed highway. The cost of the additional construction was $507 million. Because the bids included the obligation to carry out additional construction, it is not possible to determine how the winning consortium would have valued only the 69 kilometres of the highway that the government had completed. But, had the government spent the $507 million to complete the highway itself, it is reasonable to assume that the winning consortium would have paid approximately $3.6 billion for it.

Thus, the entire project still would have been valued at $1.6 billion more than the government's total cost of $2 billion. The project generated a net present value that greatly exceeded the government's initial investment, and the cost overrun pales into insignificance relative to that net present value. (We are not arguing here that the government maximized the return on its investment by the form of privatization undertaken in 1999 – as discussed below, we think it did not – but rather that the privatization demonstrated that the net present value of the project was clearly positive.) Thus, evaluating Highway 407 as a technology and construction project from a net present value standpoint, it was a great success.

The fact that the Standish criterion (on time completion within budget and with full functionality) and the net present value criterion deliver different evaluations of Highway 407 as a project should give us pause. The Standish Group criterion is defined in producer terms, rather than in terms of the interaction between the project's cost to produce and value to end users. It is possible to have a project delivered on time, on budget, and with full functionality, that does not gain user acceptance and hence has a negative net present value. Conversely, a project could be over budget, late, and delivered with less than full functionality but still be embraced by users and hence have a positive net present value. Net present value, by incorporating a measure of value to users – and an accurate measure, given that highway 407 is a toll road – takes into account both value to users and cost to producers. Our conclusion is that, at least in this case, it was a more accurate criterion than that of the Standish Group.[2]

This measure of success for Highway 407 seems to have escaped Joan Boase (1999), the only academic who has discussed it to date. She noted that the highway was late, thereby missing anticipated revenue, and that the modifications recommended by the safety review increased cost (Boase 1999, 86). In her discussion of privatization, she was surprised that the purchaser did not require safeguards, for example either guaranteed traffic volume, or lower speed limits on competing highways. What Boase did not realize was that the project was sufficiently valuable to drivers that the consortium did not need to ask for such safeguards; rather, it was the province that requested safeguards to ensure that a profit-maximizing purchaser did not react to inelastic demand by increasing tolls so drastically that traffic levels dropped.

We conclude, therefore, that Highway 407 was a successful project. How was this success achieved? We believe that the key factors were good leadership and good management. The following sections explain why.

THE ROLE OF LEADERSHIP

The UK Parliamentary Office of Science and Technology (2003) report on managing large IT projects emphasizes the role of leadership. In addition to effective leadership of the project itself, the report cites senior management commitment. Thus, it recommends that projects have a senior champion, a senior public servant to whom the project manager reports and who is responsible for the project's ultimate success. While this report seems to speak mainly about leadership within the public service, it is clear that if a project is as high-profile and, at times, as controversial as Highway 407, it also needs strong and committed political leadership. The record shows that Highway 407 had strong leadership at both levels.

The political leadership of the Rae government initiated the development of Highway 407 as a toll highway. Premier Rae took a lead role in championing the project, publicly as well as within the government. He was enthusiastically supported by Minister Pouliot. The project broke with tradition in the Ontario government, and presented political hurdles too. A toll highway and partnership with the private sector were both novel and controversial developments for the NDP, and support within the cabinet and the caucus was not automatic. When turf battles threatened the project, as when the Ministry of Finance attempted to weaken the OTCC, the Premier intervened decisively.

Initially, the project chugged along within the MTO bureaucracy. There was little resistance to it, but neither was there any great sense of urgency. The appointment of George Davies as deputy minister of transportation changed that. He put the project into overdrive and was able to bring the initial stages of contract award and negotiation to successful completion. It is the consensus of most observers that Highway 407 would not have been delivered nearly as fast as it was, had Davies not been placed in charge.

As noted earlier, a close working relationship between the minister's staff and the senior civil servants at MTO and the consequent informal briefings and discussions that preceded formal decisions also contributed to streamlined decision-making.

Finally, by accelerating the project, the government stood to reap obvious benefits from job creation and relief of traffic congestion. There was a conscious effort by the Premier and Minister Pouliot, however, to ignore partisan political considerations when making decisions about the highway. The appointment of the external members of the OTCC board provides the clearest example. None of the appointees had any previous relationship with the NDP. The principles of employment equity, which were dear to the Rae government, were not followed, as discussed earlier. The board members were chosen for their expertise, as well as for their ability to withstand a change of government, as indeed they did.

Consider also decision-making and selection. The cabinet made policy decisions, but the civil service made the final decision on the bid selection. This was a conscious decision by the cabinet to insulate itself from allegations of political interference. While there was political controversy around the contract award, it turned out to be unsubstantiated, as the incoming Harris government discovered on assuming office. Had there been any substance to it, the new government could have suspended the project while carrying out an inquiry. They could even have tried to cancel it, as the Chretien government did in the case of the Pearson airport privatization. In any case, the potential for delay was there. That it did not happen is a further indication of the meticulous processes and careful decision-making of the Rae government and the committee of deputy ministers, during the initial stages of the project.

This depoliticization of Highway 407 illustrates an interesting paradox. Politicians want to leave programs or projects as their legacies. The challenge all politicians face is that, inevitably, and often very soon, they will be succeeded by politicians of another party. One effective way to prevent one's successors from destroying one's legacy is to make it possible for them to embrace, or at least accept, it. This argues for depoliticizing a project so that one's successors can accept it on its merits alone, rather than reject it because of its association with *their* predecessors.

As the project moved from initiation to implementation, and from the Rae to Harris governments, it continued to receive strong bureaucratic and political leadership. Both George Davies and his successor Jan Rush saw delivering Highway 407 as a major personal priority and component of their performance contracts. While neither micromanaged the project, they were both available to Dennis Galange and gave full attention at critical moments. For example, they both put pressure on their counterparts at Hughes Aircraft and Bell Canada to make sure the necessary resources were devoted to delivering the tolling technology without additional delay. They also advised the minister on issues management, for example the safety issue, with a level of political sensitivity that one would not expect of a project manager with a private sector background. At the political level, Minister Palladini was as committed as his predecessor Minister Pouliot to delivering the highway. In addition, given his background as the owner of a very successful automobile dealership, he took an active interest in and made suggestions regarding the marketing of the highway.

To summarize, successful leadership on this project required a mix of passion for it and distance from it. The passion on the part of Rae, Pouliot, Palladini, Davies, and Rush was to make it a personal priority, to allocate scarce time to it, to argue for it with outside stakeholders, and, when necessary, to put pressure on private sector contractors. Rae, Pouliot, and Palladini all exercised good judgment, however, in knowing when not to be involved and what to delegate to public servants.

OTCC AS A TOOL FOR PROJECT MANAGEMENT

This section discusses OTCC as a tool for project management in terms of its structural features and its strengths and weaknesses in that role. While OTCC had the legal status of a Crown corporation, it had many of the characteristics of a federal government service agency (such as Canada Customs and Revenue Agency or Parks Canada), or of what the UK government calls a next steps agency (Zussman 2002). These included increased managerial and financial autonomy, recruitment of staff with special skills from either the OPS or externally, and external directors. Dennis Galange, the President of OTCC, brought expertise from the private sector in corporate finance and project management. David Garner, an experienced public servant was seconded from MTO to oversee the engineering and construction aspects of the project, and he was advised by Delcan Associates, the consulting engineers who monitored the construction process.

Dennis Galange saw this organizational structure as well-fitted to its mission. He described OTCC as a "great project management structure, a high profile team that was different from the ministry. Some had private sector backgrounds and those with public sector backgrounds thought like private sector managers. The people worked very hard and were passionate in their commitment to the highway."[3] David Guscott, Transportation ADM for Policy and Planning at the time, agreed that OTCC was a good project management organization, with a great deal of expertise. He also concluded that having a board with a substantial number of external directors created a different dynamic than he had experienced at Crown corporations with internal boards. OTCC staff had an extra measure of accountability, having to justify their actions to the outside directors, and the outside directors could also offer advice to staff.[4]

Consider this hypothetical but not implausible scenario of how an agency with an external board could create a dynamic different from the traditional departmental administration. Assume that during the highway's free use period the government contemplated increasing its popularity with drivers, especially those living in the politically important 905 area code, by abandoning tolls. Likely some external board members would have argued passionately that this was bad public policy. They might have threatened to resign and publicly denounce the minister and, if the minister persisted, could have made good on their threat. If the minister and cabinet felt that the electoral calculus justified abandoning tolls, they would have done it. Still, an ex ante threat of opposition from a board member would have had more influence than the prospect of ex post criticism by unrelated commentators. By appointing a board of knowledgeable outsiders, the government had at least internalized points of view that it might otherwise have ignored.

An additional source of strength for OTCC was its commitment to risk management as a tool for disciplined thinking. Given the substantial risk the government was accepting, risk management was essential. Risks were identified and, for each, staff assessed the probability it would occur, rated its seriousness in terms of its consequences, and discussed how to mitigate it. Risks were tracked from one board meeting to another. The risk management framework provided an impetus for OTCC to develop contingency plans in the early months of 1997, a particularly dark period for management when it appeared possible that the technology would not work with full functionality.

Despite OTCC's many strengths as a project management organization, it displayed some weaknesses. Because a small and elite organization was given responsibility for the largest and most exciting road transportation project in recent Ontario history, it incurred the resentment of staff at MTO. We have not been able to determine, however, if resentment led to covert opposition, for example in supporting the raising of questions about safety by members of the OPP. In any event, if there was covert opposition, it did not derail the project.

The establishment of a Crown corporation with a project management mission raises human resource management issues. The individuals who were seconded from MTO to OTCC bought into the excitement and single-minded purpose of a high-profile project. Especially at the senior level, they staked their reputations on the success of the project, in terms of both outputs and process. At middle management and the front lines, they gave up the security of being in touch with their home ministry. Those who did return found a ministry that was in the process of a major downsizing, and this undoubtedly affected their career prospects. In general, uncertainty about the situation upon return will discourage secondment to priority projects. The OPS currently has a corporate initiative focused on project management, which is seeking ways to overcome a variety of systemic barriers with human resource policies and practices that are more supportive of project work.

Finally, under the NDP Government, OTCC started out with a broad mandate that included transportation financing and policy development. The Harris government narrowed its mandate to the development of Highway 407, and it was likely that this greater focus contributed to its success. Nonetheless, there are important transportation issues in the GTA that extend beyond any one ministry or government, and call for horizontal solutions. As a consequence, as part of its growth plan for the Greater Golden Horseshoe, the McGuinty government is proposing to "establish the Greater Toronto Transportation Authority to support the ongoing development of an integrated transportation system across the region" (Ministry of Public Infrastructure Renewal 2004c, 35). From an organizational perspective, this illustrates one of the difficulties of service or next steps agencies: they are more effective at working on focused problems, such as delivering a highway, than on horizontal issues, such as planning multimodal transportation infrastructure for a major metropolitan area.

If we judge OTCC in terms of its core competency, project management, our judgment is very positive. The OECD (2001) report on managing major IT projects, written two years after OTCC was wound up, attempted to define best practice in project management. Ontario's experience with Highway 407 is consistent with most of the recommendations in the OECD report. The recommendations include

- identifying and managing risk, as shown by OTCC's risk management methodology

- having clear lines of accountability. (Accountability for Highway 407 went from the President of OTCC, to the deputy minister as chair of the board, to the minister as shareholder.)

- recruiting well-qualified talent, as shown by OTCC's mix of internal and external expertise

- providing incentives and penalties for contractor performance, as indicated by the $6 million early completion bonus CHIC received and the $1 million penalty for lateness the Bell Canada/Bell Sygma/Hughes consortium paid

- involving end users in project design, as accomplished by a series of comprehensive traffic surveys and forecasts.

Interestingly, the OECD report recommended avoiding emerging technologies and favouring standard rather than custom software. Highway 407's integration of transponders and videoimaging was, of course, leading-edge technology requiring specialized software. The fact that the project succeeded implies that project management practices were sufficiently strong to meet the challenge of delivering an emerging technology.

FAIRNESS AND TRANSPARENCY

The issues of fairness and transparency are complicated ones for large projects. Consider fairness first. Such projects represent major business opportunities and putting together consortia to bid on them is time-consuming and expensive. Bidders often believe that lobbying will help them win, and therefore hire government relations consultants. Fairness issues concern appropriate management of the process, particularly constraints regarding lobbying either politicians or public servants.

The key issue in terms of transparency is whether the contract that is signed with the winning bidder will be made public. Contracts for projects like Highway 407 are complicated and detailed, often hundreds of pages long. Scholars (Boase 1999) and commentators claim that the public has the right to see such contracts because they deal with major public sector initiatives. This might well constrain what the government and the bidder would agree to. One additional reason for making contracts public is to forestall controversy. Once interest in and speculation about their terms has been raised, government clearly benefits from showing that it has nothing to hide. Bidders, however, have resisted attempts to make contracts public, arguing that this would be injurious in revealing proprietary information to competitors who would also be bidding on future projects. Some potential bidders might refuse to participate if the winning bid is made public, which would reduce competition.

The distinction between easiest case (low complexity, high contestability, low asset specificity) and most difficult case (high complexity, low contestability, high asset specificity) procurement is relevant to this discussion. When purchasing standard goods, the government defines the specifications and calls for sealed bids. Competition is on the basis of price alone, and the lowest qualified bidder wins the contract. Politicians are not involved in the process at all. With regard to transparency, the public policy purpose in releasing the price of the winning bid is to encourage bidders in the next competition to better the price. This is done in some jurisdictions, typically on their procurement websites. In industries that have had a history of collusion, notably construction, announcing all bids publicly is seen as a way to undercut it.

Procurement in the most difficult case involves more challenging issues of due process and transparency. In the original procurement decisions for the highway and technology, the NDP Government hired Price Waterhouse as consultants to oversee the process and refused to permit any contact between ministers and bidders. It then went a step farther in depoliticizing the process by delegating responsibility for reviewing bids to a committee of deputy ministers. The committee, and not the cabinet, chose one consortium's proposal for the road and the other consortium's technology.

Matters became more complicated for the NDP after the decision was made. The losing consortium (ORDC) was very disappointed, particularly because they had made the initial proposal to build the highway, and had formed before the winners (CHIC). The government kept the proposals and evaluation documents secret after the decision was taken because the final contract had not yet been negotiated with CHIC, and because both bidders wanted secrecy. MTO Deputy Minister George Davies and ADM David Guscott would have liked to provide an in depth post-award briefing to ORDC so they would understand the legitimate reasons why their proposal had not been accepted. With ORDC threatening to sue the government at the time, the legal advice was not to provide such a briefing. In retrospect, both Davies and Guscott thought a post-award briefing would have been a good idea. One way to facilitate it would have been to require bidders to include a signed contract with their bid. This would have expedited contract negotiations, so that the post-award briefing could have been provided sooner. The NDP government made available to the public a summary of the main provisions of the construction contract, and provided the complete contract to the Provincial Auditor.[5]

Despite some similarities, the privatization process followed by the Conservatives differed markedly from the NDP's procurement process. The Harris government also retained a process consultant (PricewaterhouseCoopers, the successor to Price Waterhouse) and the bid document did prohibit discussion of bids with members of cabinet. We have been told, however, that the Conservative cabinet was not as zealous as the NDP in avoiding contact with bidders. Unlike the NDP's procurement process, Conservative politicians made the key decisions about privatization. Though the identity of the bidders was hidden from ministers on the Cabinet Committee on Privatization, they did not ask for a recommendation from the bureaucracy. Ministers chose one of four options for the eastern terminus of the highway, and decided to have the two highest bidders rebid on Option 1 (completing the eastern extension of the highway to Brock Road). The Privatization Secretariat subsequently determined the winner on the basis of price alone.

When the contract was signed, the Harris government and 407 International mutually agreed to keep it confidential, though investors and rating agencies were permitted to obtain copies by signing confidentiality agreements. The government released a summary of the contract. When requests for the entire contract were made under the Freedom of Information Act, 407 International objected to its release on the grounds that it contained personal and business sensitive information. When these concerns were satisfied, the concession agreement was released in early 2003 by the Eves government, which had taken office by that time. The question of whether to release major contracts remains a contentious one. While 407 International's grounds for objecting to the document's release appear reasonable, it took almost four years for the contract to be available to the public, sans the offending sections. The McGuinty government, as part of its democratic renewal agenda, appears to be taking the position that all major procurement contracts should be made public, but this position has yet to be tested in a particular case.

Looking back at both the procurement and privatization processes, we draw several conclusions. In our system of Cabinet government, Cabinet has the right to decide who will receive major government contracts. In the past, that often meant awarding contracts explicitly on the basis of past political loyalty (rewarding your friends) or promises of future support, such as donations. Public attitudes have changed to the point that such behaviour is now considered corrupt. Politicians have responded to this change in public values in a number of ways. As a first step, governments are prohibiting ministers from being lobbied by individual bidders and threatening to disqualify bidders who attempt to lobby ministers. As a second step, when it comes time for ministers to choose among proposals, the identity of the proponents is being masked.[6] Going one step further, some governments, such as Rae's, will decide only on the major features of the project, and leave the actual choice among competing proposals to the bureaucracy.

Even if all these steps have been taken to depoliticize the process, major contracts will still be the subject of public discussion and debate. Debate requires information, and therefore, we support greater transparency by making contracts public. We do not find convincing the argument that some potential bidders might refuse to participate if details of the winning bid are made public. We find it difficult to believe that potential bidders would forgo the opportunity to participate in a project that is worth several hundreds of millions of dollars for this reason.

4. THE APPROPRIATENESS OF TOLLS

Tolls on Highway 407 have frequently been criticized as too high. There are two versions of this argument. The more radical is that Highway 407 should have no tolls at all, that it should be a traditional freeway. The less radical version is that tolls are acceptable, but the current level is too high. We will examine both.

The argument that Highway 407 should have been a traditional freeway was certainly in the minds of drivers during its free use period from June to October 1997. With Highway 407 accommodating 350,000 daily trips, Highway 401 was less congested than it had been in decades, and drivers on both highways, if asked, would undoubtedly have voted to preserve this happy state of affairs. The argument that 407 should have stayed a freeway was made for financial reasons by writer Jay Teitel (1998) in *Toronto Life*,

> [E]ven if the 407 saved only half the current claimed congestion deficit [i.e. the cost of congestion to the Toronto economy, as estimated by OTCC], one billion dollars, it would still take just a couple of years to save enough money to effectively pay for the cost of the highway. In fact, you'd save so much money every year that the amount flowing into tax revenues would far exceed the amount you'd collect in tolls, which were just there to pay for the highway in the first place.

The argument for not tolling Highway 407 derives from the economic theory of the second best (Borins 1984). That theory argues that if economic distortions (for example, prices not equal to marginal social cost) already exist and cannot be removed, say for political reasons, economic welfare (defined as the difference between what people are willing to pay for goods and services and the cost to society of producing those goods and services) may actually be increased by creating off-setting distortions. The application to highways in Toronto is as follows. Highway 401 is already congested. During busy periods, which now encompass much of the day, its implicit price (the cost of driving on the highway, in terms of time and money, for the average driver) is less than its marginal cost (the additional delay created for all other drivers by one more driver).[7] Highway 407 is a substitute for Highway 401, so by pricing it in the same way as Highway 401 – a freeway without tolls – as much traffic as possible would be shifted from Highway 401 to it, and economic welfare would be increased. This argument is technically correct.

Teitel's financial argument that even without tolls Highway 407 would pay for itself is incorrect. The cost of congestion on Highway 401 is mainly wasted time and gasoline. Opening Highway 407 shifted some drivers from Highway 401 and reduced wasted time and gasoline for drivers still using Highway 401, but that in itself did not bring in any new tax revenues that could be used to pay for Highway 407.

There are two arguments for tolling Highway 407 that, in our view, override second best economics. First, Ontario had been rapidly accumulating public debt since 1990, and the government had public support in its efforts to control that debt. OTCC was frequently made aware that the capital markets were watching closely and, if the government could or would not implement tolls, they would immediately add $1.5 billion to Ontario's debt load. The Balanced Budget and Taxpayer Protection Act, which was passed by the Harris government, can be seen as an indication of public aversion to government deficits that add to the debt load. Secondly, urban sprawl is a major problem in Toronto, as in many other cities (Jacobs 2004, Ministry of Public Infrastructure Renewal 2004c). Building more freeways exacerbates the problem. One way to have cities consume less space is to force drivers to pay tolls that represent the marginal social cost of traffic congestion, which includes both delay and pollution. Cities that consume less space will have higher population densities, which supports public transit. Public transit riders produce less pollution and congestion per capita than do drivers. From this perspective, Highway 407 can be seen as a first step in using state-of-the-art technology to gain public acceptance for road pricing. We feel that the argument for using tolls on Highway 407 as a first step toward using road pricing to reduce urban sprawl overrides a second best economics argument that is predicated on accepting an undesirable status quo.[8]

The next step in reducing sprawl would be tolling existing highways and urban streets, for example by imposing tolls on cars entering the downtown core during peak hours, and allocating the revenues derived from tolls to cover the cost of improvements in public transit. The most significant recent initiative in road pricing was undertaken by the municipal government of London, England, which, on February 17, 2003, imposed a toll of 5 pounds on vehicles entering a 20-square kilometre congestion charge zone in the central city between 7 a.m. and 6:30 p.m. on weekdays. The technology used has 700 cameras videoimaging all cars entering the zone and then matching the images against a database of vehicles whose drivers have paid tolls in advance. Escalating fines for unpaid trips begin the same evening. The electronic tolling technology is working well; traffic delays within the congestion charge zone have decreased by about 30 %, and in the first year the tolls brought in net revenues of approximately 70 million pounds, which will be used to improve public transit (Cappe 2004, Hutton 2003, Freeman and Lewington 2003, Kennedy 2003). London's transport agency is now considering extending road tolling beyond the urban core (Clement 2004). While this technology is impressive, it is still less advanced than that of Highway 407. The latter integrates both videoimaging and transponders; each car without a transponder is imaged twice, once entering and once leaving the highway, rather than once, as is the practice in London.

Partly in reaction to London's experience, the imposition of road tolls has entered public debate in Toronto. Tolls have been advocated by urban planner Joe Berridge (2003) and newspaper columnist John Barber (2003). Then mayoral candidate, now Toronto mayor, David Miller stated that in the absence of additional provincial government funding for public transit he would consider imposing tolls on two freeways, the Don Valley Parkway and Gardiner Expressway. This conditional endorsement of tolls was attacked by the other candidates, most notably John Tory, who, during the campaign posted a website condemning Miller's position on tolls.[9] A few months after the municipal election, the TTC received major funding commitments from the provincial and federal governments. The province provided $90 million in immediate funding to avert a fare increase (Lewington and Campbell

2004). The federal, provincial, and Toronto governments agreed to a five-year total commitment of $1 billion that includes modernization and infrastructure improvements for the subway, streetcars, and buses (Premier of Ontario 2004). While these commitments relieve the immediate pressure on Mayor Miller, they will not fund major transit expansion, such as the construction of new subway lines (Barber 2004). Road tolling, however, has the potential to provide additional revenue for major investments in transit, and we expect it to continue to remain a topic of public debate.

The soft argument regarding tolls, namely that current tolls are in some sense too high, is based on the actual increases in tolls since Highway 407 was privatized. It takes as an implicit comparison the NDP's original tolling policy, which was that tolls would pay for the highway and then, once the highway was paid for and its debt retired, be removed. OTCC made this policy more detailed, specifying a period of 30 years to pay down the original debt, as well as ongoing maintenance and additional investment over that period. The Conservatives' approach differed markedly, privatizing the revenue stream from the highway, with the purchasers obligated to provide ongoing maintenance and additional investment. The McGuinty government's approach combines an acceptance of the concessionaire's right to charge tolls under the Conservatives' contract, with a reinterpretation of the contract to the effect that the government must agree to toll levels, thus attempting to slow their rate of increase.[10]

Comparing the trajectories tolls would likely follow under the NDP and Conservative approaches is an economics problem beyond the scope of our book. We can at least say that, if the NDP approach were followed, tolls would disappear after thirty years, in 2027, and the highway would revert to public ownership and maintenance, like the rest of the provincial highway system. In contrast, the privatization approach would maintain tolls until 2098. Calculating tolls in the first thirty years under the NDP approach would require assumptions about the highway's capital structure (that is, its mixture of equity and debt of varying maturities), any regulated constraints on the rate of return on equity, and the factors, such as population and income growth and price elasticity, influencing demand for the highway over time.[11] From this it would be possible to derive various sets of tolls by vehicle category that would produce revenues sufficient to cover maintenance, additional investment, and debt retirement. One set of tolls would have to be chosen from all the feasible sets. A political calculus would also enter the picture since the cabinet had to approve tolls. It is possible to visualise a scenario where the cabinet, in an election year, could refuse to approve requested toll increases. Finally, this set of tolls would be compared to those predicted under the privatization approach, using comparable assumptions regarding demand but different assumptions regarding capital structure.

There have been substantial toll increases since the highway was privatized. Peak period tolls for cars, trucks, and trailer trucks all increased by 29.5% in the first four years since the highway was privatized (from $.10 to $.1295 per kilometre for cars, $.20 to $.259 per kilometre for trucks, and $.30 to $.3885 per kilometre for trailer trucks). Over the same period, the charge per trip for drivers not using transponders increased from $2 to $3.30, an increase of 65%.

Where toll increases have been greatest is off-peak. For example, when the highway was privatized there was a mid-day off-peak toll and a lower, overnight off-peak toll. The overnight toll disappeared, so now there is only one off-peak rate, which applies to weekdays from 10 a.m. to 3 p.m., evenings from 7 p.m. to 6 a.m., weekends, and holidays. The mid-day off-peak rates for cars, trucks, and trailer trucks rose by 73% in the first four years following privatization (from $.07 to $.1210 per kilometre for cars, $.14 to $.242 per kilometre for trucks, and $.21 to $.363 per kilometre for trailer trucks). From May 2000 until February 2003, off-peak tolls were the same as peak period tolls. 407 International does not publish usage statistics by type of traffic or time of day. Assuming that it is a profit-maximizing firm, it increased off-peak tolls so much because it believed off-peak trips are not very sensitive to the price charged.

In February 2003, 407 International increased off-peak tolls slightly less than peak-period tolls, so that there is now a very small differential, for example a peak rate of $.1295 per kilometre for cars compared to $.1210 per kilometre off-peak. Peak and off-peak tolls by vehicle type are shown in the table on page 123. Their rationale was to provide more information about the impact of differential toll rates on demand (407 International 2004).

While tolls have increased, traffic levels have continued to grow as well. For example, the average number of weekday trips increased from 239,000 in May 1999, when the highway was privatized, to 317,000 in May 2003, an increase of 33%. Part of this increase is due to continuing extension of the highway. When Highway 407 was opened, the traffic modelling done by Wilbur Smith Associates indicated that the tolls put in place in 1997 would maximize revenue – if tolls were any higher, traffic

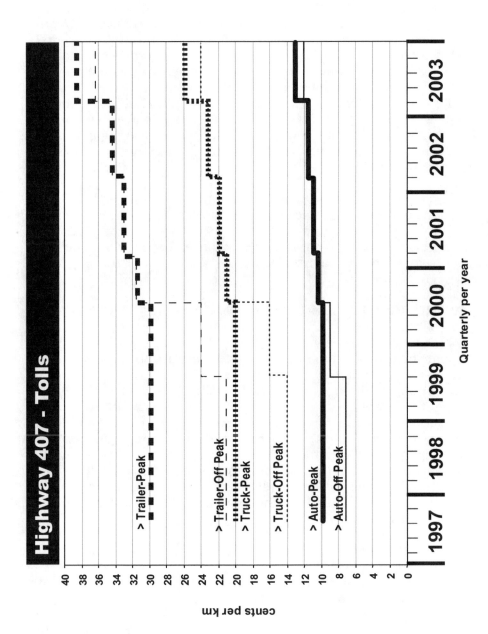

would decline so much that revenue would also fall. The increase in trips since 1997 indicates that the demand for travel on Highway 407 was stronger than forecast by Wilbur Smith, with the consequence that 407 International has been able to increase tolls substantially from the 1997 level. Similarly, the safeguards built into the privatization contract were intended to prohibit 407 International from increasing tolls so much that traffic would decline, but the company has been able to increase tolls substantially without being constrained by the safeguards. Still, 407 International argues that tolls are not excessive compared to similar electronic toll roads in the US. They cite a number of such roads in California, Virginia, Texas, Florida, and Delaware that charge between $.10 and $.20 in Canadian dollars per kilometre at peak periods (http://www.407etr.com).

The question of the appropriateness of tolls is directly linked to the evaluation of privatization, since the level of tolls has a direct impact on the profitability of the highway, and as a consequence both the price a concessionaire would pay for it and the value of the privatized asset over time. It is to this question we now turn.

ALTERNATIVES TO THE PRIVATIZATION CONTRACT

We come back to the conclusions we drew in the previous chapter about the privatization of Highway 407. Privatization was intended to produce maximum short-term revenue for the Harris government, and its timing was dictated by the 1999 election campaign. From the Harris government's point of view, the privatization was a great success. It was hailed at the time as a good deal for the taxpayer and enabled the government simultaneously to continue cutting taxes, balance the budget, and increase spending on health, an area of great public concern. While Highway 407 itself was not an election issue, and was rarely mentioned during the campaign, the contribution it made to the province's finances helped re-elect the Harris government.

Viewing the privatization from a long-term perspective, however, we criticized this approach for several reasons. First, the Harris government left money on the table: the value of the highway had grown to between $8 and $13 billion in four years, but it gave up any share in this increment. Second, the Harris government leased the highway for ninety-nine years, an unconscionably long term. Third, by foregoing an offer to extend the highway east to its natural terminus, Highway

35/115, the Harris government has increased the difficulty its successors will face in contracting for that extension.

The Canadian Council for Public-Private Partnerships (2000, 18) gave the privatization of Highway 407 its gold award for financial partnerships. The main reason for the award was that a deal of this magnitude – the largest privatization in Canadian history – "mov[ed] from concept to final sale in less than a year." The award also noted the economic benefits created: congestion relief for the GTA, six thousand person-years of construction work in extending the highway from 69 to 108 kilometres, and CHIC's winning the contract to build the Cross-Israel toll highway. We find these reasons unconvincing. We think the haste with which the deal was done contributed to its weakness in the long term. Congestion relief preceded privatization; in fact, it was what made Highway 407 attractive to bidders. Finally, CHIC's entire involvement with Highway 407 preceded the privatization. As we will discuss below, keeping the highway in public hands would have done more for CHIC's ability to export technology.

In our view, there were two major alternatives to the Harris government's approach to privatization: privatization for the long term, and public ownership. We will outline both below, and show why we think either one would have been preferable to the approach followed by the Harris government. We believe that analyzing these options is not merely an exercise in Monday-morning quarterbacking because the decision makers at the time were at least aware of these options. They explicitly rejected an initial purchase offering (IPO) that would have implemented the long-term privatization approach, and their ideological views regarding the public sector led' them to give short shrift to public ownership.

PRIVATIZATION FOR THE LONG TERM

In this approach, the government would still have leased the operation of the highway, but it would have done so with a much greater emphasis on long-term benefits and eventualities. The government would have accepted the Woodbridge Company's offer to complete Highway 407 east to Highways 35/115 (Option 4). Rather than leasing the highway for 99 years, it would have offered a shorter term, say 30 years. As discussed in chapter 8, the Privatization Secretariat's tactic of indicative bidding gave the bidders an incentive to exaggerate the difference between what they would offer for a 99-year lease and what they would offer for a 30-year lease. We estimate the difference would actually be on the order of $100 million relative to total offers of $3 billion. The difference of $100 million is the net present value of all profits from 31 to 99 years in the future. Because these profits are discounted at a rate that represents the bidders' opportunity cost of capital, their value today (i.e. their present value) becomes very small.

There is an irony here that should not escape the reader. One of the assumed differences between public and private sector decision-making is that the public sector, which is expected to represent the interests of future generations, should be more cognizant of the distant future than the private sector. In financial terms, this would mean that the public sector operates with a lower discount rate than the private sector. A more sceptical interpretation of public sector decision-making would be that politicians' time horizons are no longer than the end of their mandates, so that the Harris government's time horizon for deciding in 1999 about Highway 407 privatization was only a few months.[12] We believe the nature of the privatization is more supportive of the sceptical interpretation.

Had the Harris government accepted the Woodbridge Company's offer for Option 4 and leased the highway for 30 years, it would have received $2.7 billion (the $2.8 billion offered by Woodbridge for a 99-year lease less $100 million). This is $400 million less than it actually received. Assume that, extrapolating from Highway 407's success from its opening in October 1997 to early 1999, the government thought there was a reasonable probability that the value of the highway would increase as the market also came to see its potential. The government could have taken advantage of this potential by retaining an interest in the highway. Thus, it would have leased a majority interest in the project, maintaining a minority interest for itself. It would have had to make clear that it would be a passive investor, with a commitment not to infringe upon the majority investor's decisions any more than it did in the actual privatization agreement. In effect, the government would agree to play a role similar to SNC-Lavalin, which now holds 16% of the shares of 407 International. This would also be analogous to an investor who sells part of his holdings in a stock that is increasing in price to lock in some profits, but keeps the rest in the expectation of additional profits.

There are two ways the government could have structured the deal. It could have used the money it received for a majority share in the project to retire the $1.5 billion in debt it had incurred to build the highway, and then put its equity in the highway on its books as an investment. It would then have been able to show the value of this investment increasing over time, and to use annual dividends towards its operating budget.

Possibly a more attractive approach from the Harris government's perspective in 1999 would have been to put the cash it would have received for the majority share in the highway toward the annual budget and to use its equity in the highway to cover the debt it had incurred to build the road. Thus the cash could have gone to reducing the deficit and increasing health care spending, both of which it considered to be politically more attractive than retiring debt. Using the equity to cover the debt still achieves the original goal of building the highway without incurring additional debt.[13]

The long-term privatization approach therefore achieves the Harris government's immediate political objective – producing revenue to balance the budget and fund health care – while also achieving the long-term objectives of participating in the increasing value of the highway, completing it eastwards to Highway 35/115, and reducing the term of the lease.

PUBLIC OWNERSHIP OF HIGHWAY 407

The Privatization Secretariat expressed very well the Harris Conservatives' attitude towards government. It assumed mismanagement was endemic to government, and preferred private ownership wherever possible. Apart from its electoral calculus, it had a strong ideological reason for divesting itself of the highway as soon as possible. This, of course, is not the only possible perspective on public ownership. Proponents of public ownership (for example Hardin 1974) argue that Crown corporations have built a great deal of Canada's infrastructure and have done it with a level of economic efficiency roughly comparable to the private sector. From this perspective, the Ontario government's investment in a successful toll road using the world's most advanced technology was an opportunity to be exploited, rather than hastily divested.

The divesting of the Ontario Transportation Capital Corporation, therefore, is a story of missed opportunity, similar to that of the disposition of Research Enterprises Limited after World War II (Borins 1983). Research Enterprises was a Crown corporation, based in Toronto, which had developed expertise in the production of radar and optical glass. Then Minister of Munitions and Supply C.D. Howe mistakenly believed that there were bleak postwar prospects for these products and had the corporation dismantled and sold. A more hopeful variation on this theme is Teranet, a Toronto-based partnership between the Ontario Government and a private sector consortium that automated Ontario's land registry system and developed leading-edge software (Daniels and

Scrivens 1997). The partnership had been in operation since 1991, had automated a substantial proportion of Ontario's land records, had developed new software, and had exported its technology and expertise. The Eves government sold Ontario's 50 percent share in Teranet to the consortium in August 2003 for $370 million, by which time Teranet had become a more mature enterprise. The sale returned the government a profit of approximately $100 million on a total investment of about $250 million. Less than a year later, however, the McGuinty government is considering reacquiring Teranet at a substantially higher price than the Eves government received (Reguly 2004).

Had the government decided to retain Highway 407 in the public sector, the story could have played out in the following way. Ontario Transportation Capital Corporation would have remained a Crown corporation, but it would have been structured along the lines of the Liquor Control Board of Ontario. It would have had an openly commercial objective of maximizing profit. This could have been done by appointing a board of directors primarily external to the government, appointing someone other than the deputy minister of transportation as chair of the board, and by requiring the minister to issue public directives if (s)he wished to countermand the board. Another way to increase managerial autonomy would be for OTCC to issue shares through an initial purchase offering (IPO), which, while bringing in revenue for the government, would also have the effect of creating minority shareholders whose objective would be to maximize the value of their investment, and who would therefore exert pressure on management to maximize profit. This option was considered by the Harris government, but rejected in favour of the long-term lease.

After completing construction of the initial 69 kilometres of Highway 407, OTCC would have continued to contract out construction and tolling for the remainder of the highway, and, assuming the environmental assessment process was successful, it would have completed the eastern part of the highway through to Highway 35/115.

OTCC could have capitalized on its expertise in tolling technology and highway construction. Working from its experience tolling Highway 407, OTCC could have begun examining technological options for tolling other highways in the 400 series or for tolling urban streets. Decisions to implement tolls are inherently political; we discuss the rationale for tolling in the final section of this chapter. Still, OTCC could have begun the analytical work that would inform such decisions. It could also have worked on "smart" highways as well as other uses for transponder technology. As pointed out by the Canadian Council for Public-Private Partnerships, CHIC's experience with Highway 407 led to it winning the contract for the Cross-Israel Toll Highway. Retaining OTCC as a Crown corporation could have made it and its partners strong contenders for contracts for major highways and tolling systems throughout the world; one of the original objectives of the Rae government. Highway 407 could therefore have been used as a springboard to create a Canadian presence of global significance in state-of-the art highway and transportation development. That opportunity has been lost; instead, Highway 407 has become the fourteenth toll road owned and operated by the Spanish company Cintra Concesiones de Infraestructuras de Transporte, a major investment for the Australian financier Macquarrie Infrastructure Group, and a profitable passive investment for SNC-Lavalin (De Cloet 2003).

Unfortunately, the public ownership option has been foreclosed. Ultimately, Highway 407 will stand as an instance of more or less constrained private profit maximization – depending on the outcome of the legal dispute between the McGuinty government and 407 International about tolling – in the middle of a publicly-owned transportation system.

DIRECTIONS FOR THE FUTURE

Whatever the outcome of the current dispute between the McGuinty government and 407 International, we believe that Highway 407's history suggests three directions for the future: regarding OTCC as a model for project management, enacting road tolling, and changing government's attitude towards its investments.

i) OTCC as model for project management

As we have argued earlier in this chapter, the Ontario Transportation Capital Corporation was an effective structure for managing a large public sector project, and should be used as a model for managing similar projects in the future. OTCC's key success factors included seconding to it public servants with expertise, hiring outside talent where appropriate, having supportive senior management in MTO, the department to which it reported, and incorporating the expertise and perspective provided by external directors. In addition, when the technology was behind schedule, OTCC's rigorous risk management framework helped it focus on problem solving while maintaining strategic flexibility.

To serve as a model for project management, the OTCC experience needs a bit of tweaking. The Ontario Public Service is re-examining its policies regarding both secondment of public servants and contracts for outsiders to ensure that it can hire the right talent for major projects. The external directors were chosen on the basis of their expertise, rather than political patronage. Their role also differed from that of the members of a typical public sector advisory board. The directors accepted fiduciary responsibility. The board met frequently and members were expected to read briefing books in advance. For this they were paid nominal director's fees of $200 per meeting. In contrast, advisory boards are much more informal and meet much less frequently, and members feel less obligated to attend. Often, material is not provided in advance, and members are asked to respond off-the-cuff to presentations. While adopting OTCC as a model does not necessarily require structuring a project management team as a Crown corporation with a board of directors, it does entail a more serious commitment to the use of external advisers than would be the case with a typical external advisory board. One option would be paying advisers as consultants, which the federal Auditor General does for external advisers who read and discuss drafts of chapters of its annual reports.

Choosing directors of Crown corporations, as well as other public sector agencies, on the basis of merit rather than patronage is a reform that is beginning to take hold in a number of jurisdictions. For example, the UK has an independent Commissioner for Public Appointments and British Columbia has established a Board Resourcing and Development Office (www.fin.gov.bc.ca/abc) to recruit directors whose skills and experience add value to the leadership of their organizations (Watson 2004).

One other area of concern regarding OTCC as a model is its distance from the rest of the bureaucracy. For OTCC, this appears to have led to some resentment by the bureaucracy, which perceived it as an elite organization. While a measure of resentment is likely normal, the leadership of such an organization, as well as the senior management of its host department, must make every effort to keep lines of communication open with the department and, indeed, with the rest of government.

ii) enabling road tolling

We believe there are two possible contexts for electronic road tolling: limited access highways and central cities. The technological feasibility and economic effectiveness of both has been demonstrated: the former by Highway 407 and the latter by the City of London. We would encourage transportation policy makers in Canada, in particular in the GTA – Canada's largest conurbation – to consider both. It is clear to any user of Ontario's 400-series highways that maintaining high volume expressways in a northern climate requires considerable ongoing investment in construction and maintenance. Electronic tolling of 400-series highways could cover construction and maintenance costs, allowing them to be removed from the MTO budget, thus contributing to a reduction in Ontario's deficit. (If the government's budget were in balance, tolling could finance a cut in broad-based taxes such as personal income tax.) The province is already considering using tolls to finance expansion of the 400 series highways (Mackie 2004a). As in the case of London, electronic tolling of roads leading into downtown Toronto could finance the provision of transit infrastructure.

Both the Ontario and federal governments have committed to sharing gasoline tax revenues with municipal governments. The May 2004 Ontario Budget earmarked 2.5 cents per litre of gasoline tax revenue to public transit, to be phased in by October 2006 (Minister of Finance 2004). The Liberal Party platform in the 2004 federal election promised municipalities 5 cents per litre of federal gasoline tax revenue for "major new infrastructure projects" to be phased in by 2010 (Liberal Party of Canada 2004). There is some irony in these commitments because – especially in response to criticism of the gasoline tax by the oil companies and the Canadian Automobile Association – in the past both governments have taken the position that the gasoline tax is simply an excise tax paid into the Consolidated Revenue Fund, not to be earmarked for any special purpose. If the two governments now are intending to earmark the gasoline tax at least in part for public transit it would be more efficient to impose road tolls, because tolls fall directly on those drivers who are at the heart of the urban congestion problem, namely those who drive to work downtown. The gasoline tax, on the other hand, falls on all drivers, including those who live in rural areas and others who never take their cars to work downtown.

iii) changing government's attitude towards its investments

The Harris government's attitude towards Highway 407 is a classic example of ideologically motivated thinking. Its advisers with private sector backgrounds in the Privatization Secretariat ignored the success of a public sector organization – OTCC – in delivering the highway, and, convinced that government would "screw up" any industrial venture, set about to divest the highway. It is not clear whether most of Harris's ministers shared this hard-line view, but certainly their electoral calculus led them to support the Privatization Secretariat's recommendations. The Highway 407 experience is, unfortunately, consistent with Herschel Hardin's (1974) argument that Canadians, often for the same ideological reason, are unaware of the contribution publicly owned capital has made to Canada's economic and cultural development. For us, Highway 407 stands as an example of a missed opportunity to develop leading-edge Canadian-based industry. Retaining OTCC as a Crown corporation with a commercial and developmental mission could have provided that opportunity. Such opportunities do not come often. We urge Canadian governments that have succeeded in developing new technologies with commercial potential to consider options other than privatization and, if choosing privatization, to think carefully about structuring the deal so as to enable the government to retain a long-term stake in the enterprise.

In conclusion: the story of Highway 407 is a quintessentially Canadian story of the provision of transportation infrastructure on the urban frontier. Constrained by financial exigency, and in the broad context of government reform, an NDP government acted pragmatically to solve a growing transportation problem in the GTA. It resorted to a user-pay policy and a partnership with the private sector, neither a traditional NDP approach. A Crown corporation oversaw the efforts of two private sector consortia and ultimately delivered the world's most technologically advanced highway. OTCC, together with the government, managed both the technological and market risks, and the highway opened with negligible delay and only slightly over budget. At the moment when OTCC's prospects held greatest promise, a Conservative government acted ideologically to privatize the road for a century. If we are not to repeat the mistakes we have made during our history, we must learn from them. We hope that citizens and policy-makers, particularly the McGuinty government, will learn from this experience, and do better.

APPENDIX: CHRONOLOGY

1950s	Ontario begins planning and constructing the 400 series of controlled access highways. Need for the future Highway 407 is identified. Corridor identified as part of Parkway Belt lands. Property acquisition begins.
1973	Tolls removed from the Burlington Skyway bridge, the last toll facility in Ontario.
1986	David Peterson government announces construction of Highway 407.
1987	Groundbreaking for Highway 407. Completion expected around 2020, based on existing fiscal and budgetary processes.
September 1990	NDP government takes office under Premier Bob Rae.
Spring 1992	Premier's office asks MTO to investigate viability of tolling Highway 407 to accelerate construction.
Summer 1992	Ontario Road Development Corporation (ORDC) formed. Consortium proposes to accelerate construction of Highway 407 as a toll road with a sole sourced contract.
Fall 1992	Premier's office directs MTO to develop a plan to accelerate Highway 407 as a toll road with dedicated financing.
January 1993	Premier Rae appoints George Davies Deputy Minister of Transportation.
February 1993	Policy and Priorities Board of Cabinet (P & P) meets to consider MTO's proposals on Highway 407.

	Premier Rae announces Highway 407 will be constructed as a toll facility. Invites private sector to partner with government. Canadian Highways International Corporation (CHIC) formed.
March 1993	Inter-ministerial committee created to manage the 407 process. External advisers hired.
April 1993	Minister Pouliot receives approval from P&P for toll road criteria in general and for 407 specifically.
	MTO prepares preliminary action plan. Request for qualifications (RFQ) issued. Three consortia respond.
June 1993	Decision to make the highway accessible to use not equipped with transponders.
June 24, 1993	Premier Rae announces that two consortia - OF and CHIC - have qualified to bid on the proje.
August 6, 1993	The two consortia submit value engineering studies.
September 1, 1993	Request for proposals (RFP) issued, with a December 13 deadline for submissions.
October 1993	Proposal Review Committee formed to design and oversee the evaluation process.
November 1993	Ministry of Finance presents draft of Capital Planning Act to P&P, which overrides its proposal regarding Ontario Transportation Capital Corporation (OTCC) in favour of MTO's version.
January 7, 1994	CHIC signs a no strike / no lockout labour agreement with three unions.
January 17, 1994	P&P receives progress report on the evaluation. Decides that a committee of Deputy Ministers will make the selection. P&P is concerned at request for guarantees; asks for different financing options to be considered. MTO is directed to continue letting contracts worth $150 million for construction in 1994 to insure against delays.

January 20, 1994	Labourers International Union Local 183 and two other construction unions hold biggest fundraising dinner in the NDP's history.
April 7, 1994	Deputy Ministers' committee recommends successful bidder to the Board of Directors of the OTCC.
April 8, 1994	Premier Rae and Minister Pouliot informed that CHIC has been selected. Public announcement made. All-electronic tolling system will be used and the government will negotiate with ORDC's tolling partner - the consortium of Bell Canada, Bell Sygma and Hughes Aircraft of Canada - to provide this system. The OTCC will finance the highway.
April 18, 1994	Media story attempts to link selection of CHIC to the fundraising dinner.
May 11, 1994	Negotiations with CHIC completed and contract signed.
July 25, 1994	Following discussions with MTO staff, ORDC submits unsolicited proposal to build the eastern extension of Highway 407 on an accelerated basis.
October 1994	Mike Farnan replaces Pouliot as Minister of Transportation in cabinet mini-shuffle.
December 12, 1994	MTO seeks P&P approval to accelerate 407 East and to request proposals for construction of the Western extension to the QEW. P&P directs it to return after a stakeholder consultation.
January 1995	Dennis Galange appointed CEO of the OTCC.
February 15, 1995	Farnan informs ORDC that there must be a competitive process for eastern extension of Highway 407.
February 20, 1995	P&P approves MTO's proposals originally presented on December 12, 1994.
March 31, 1995	Premier Rae announces that private sector partners are sought to accelerate planning and design for the 62 km eastern section from Highway 48 to

	Highway 35/115. Farnan makes a parallel announcement for the 22 km section west of Mississauga to the QEW in Burlington.
April 1995	RFQs are sought for both projects.
May 15, 1995	External board members are appointed to the OTCC.
June 25, 1995	Conservative government takes office under Premier Mike Harris. Al Palladini is appointed Minister of Transportation. RFQs are cancelled shortly thereafter.
September 15, 1995	OTCC signs toll system supply agreement with Bell Canada, Bell Sygma and Hughes Aircraft.
December 1995	Ontario Finance Authority issues a 30-year debenture of $500 million to cover Highway 407's accumulated construction costs.
Fall 1996	MTO initiates the environmental assessment for Highway 407 East, but only for a 15 km section from Highway 48 to Brock Road in Pickering.
October 15, 1996	Provincial Auditor releases report containing a chapter on Highway 407.
November 1996	Jan Rush appointed Deputy Minister of Transportation, replacing George Davies.
November 12, 1996	*Toronto Star* article alleges Highway 407 will be unsafe. Second article follows on November 19.
November 20, 1996	Transportation Minister Palladini announces decision to appoint independent investigator to study safety concerns.
December 31, 1996	Deadline for tolling system to be operational for drivers using transponders (missed by consortium).
March 31, 1997	Deadline for tolling system to be operational for all drivers (missed by consortium).

APPENDIX: CHRONOLOGY

April 4, 1997	Report of safety investigation conducted by Professional Engineers of Ontario (PEO) delivered to MTO.
May 1, 1997	Minister Palladini announces decision to accept all PEO recommendations.
June 7, 1997	First 39 kilometres of Highway 407 opened for free use.
October 14, 1997	Toll system operational for all drivers.
February 18, 1998	MPP Bob Wood's task force on agencies, boards and commissions identifies OTCC and Highway 407 as suitable candidates for privatization.
February 20, 1998	Minister of Privatization Rob Sampson and Minister of Transportation Tony Clement announce privatization option for Highway 407 to be explored. Process to be managed by the Privatization Secretariat.
May 1998	OTCC's External Directors' appointments allowed to lapse.
September 1, 1998	Scott Carson appointed CEO of the Privatization Secretariat.
September 4, 1998	Highway 407 opened for 69 kilometres (from Highway 403 in the west to McCowan Road in the east).
September 1998	Expressions of Interest (EOI) sought from prospective bidders for the highway, with responses due by November 27.
December 7, 1998	All four consortia that submitted EOI's are qualified to bid on the privatization.
December 10, 1998	Legislature passes Bill 70 to facilitate privatization of Highway 407 after one day of public hearings.
December 23, 1998	Privatization RFP issued, with a submission date in late February 1999. Deadline subsequently extended to March 28.

February, 1999	Lease period fixed at 99 years, following a round of indicative bids.
March 30, 1999	Cabinet Committee on Privatization presented with a blind grid of bids for different options by each consortium. Directs the two top bidders to re-bid on Option 1 only.
April 6, 1999	Final bids submitted. 407 International selected as highest bidder.
April 12, 1999	Share purchase agreement for OTCC signed (effectively privatization of highway).
May 4, 1999	Provincial budget shows $1.6 billion as net proceeds from the lease of Highway 407.
May 5, 1999	Highway 407 deal closes. Provincial election is called.
September 1999	Toll rates increase by 12%.
February 2000	Media stories about billing errors, customer service problems and erroneous licence plate denials appear.
February 21, 2000	John Ibbitson's article about the privatization and bid evaluation process published in The Globe and Mail.
February 23, 2000	Premier Harris describes vehicle registration situation as a "screw-up".
February 24, 2000	Transportation Minister David Turnbull announces suspension of licence plate denials.
April 2003	Class action on behalf of drivers who were billed late payment fees by 407 International settled. Full or partial refunds of the late fee to be made.
October 2003	Liberal government elected under Premier Dalton McGuinty on a platform that includes promise to roll back tolls on Highway 407. Announces intent to renegotiate contract with 407 International.

APPENDIX: CHRONOLOGY

February 1, 2004	407 International raises tolls despite government's objections. Government issues 407 International a notice of default.
February 9, 2004	Court rules notice of default can commence only after the dispute resolution process is completed. Government appeals this decision on April 8.
July 10, 2004	Arbitrator rules that fee increases do not have to be approved by government. Government will appeal this ruling on July 30.
July 23, 2004	407 International sues government to enforce plate denial on delinquent accounts, citing over $15 million in unpaid tolls.

REFERENCES

407 International. 2004. E-mail to the authors.

Advani, Asheesh and Borins, Sandford. 2001. "Managing Airports: A Test of the New Public Management," *International Public Management Journal* 4:1, pp. 91-107.

Babbage, Maria. 2004. "407 toll hike valid: arbitrator," *The Toronto Star*, July 11, p.1.

Barber, John. 1997. "Paying the price for a free toll highway," *The Globe and Mail*, July 30, p. A2.

Barber, John. 2000a. "Do the owners of highway 407 have a licence for this?" *The Globe and Mail*, February 8.

Barber, John. 2000b. "Toll takers unreachable, untouchable," *The Globe and Mail*, February 9.

Barber, John. 2003. "Cowardly mayoral hopefuls afraid of toll-road solution," *The Globe and Mail*, February 27.

Barber, John. 2004. "Politicians love wasting TTC money," *The Globe and Mail*, April 3, p. M2.

Berridge, Joe. 2003. "Breaking out of gridlock: there is no free road," *The Globe and Mail*, Oct. 2, p. A23.

Blakeney, Alan and Borins, Sandford. 1998. *Political Management in Canada*. 2nd ed. Toronto: University of Toronto Press.

Boase, Joan. 1999. "Beyond government? The appeal of public-private partnerships," *Canadian Public Administration* 43:1, pp. 75-92.

Borins, Sandford. 1983. "World War Two Crown Corporations: Their Functions and their Fate," pp. 447-475 in J.R.S. Prichard, ed., *Crown Corporations: The Calculus of Choice*. Toronto: Butterworth's, 1983.

Borins, Sandford. 1984. "The Economic Effects of Non-optimal Pricing and Investment Policies for Substitutable Transport Facilities," *Canadian Journal of Economics* 17:1, pp. 80-98.

Borins, Sandford. 1988a. "Electronic Road Pricing: An Idea Whose Time may Never Come," *Transportation Research* 22A:1, pp. 37-44

Borins, Sandford. 1988b. "Public Choice: 'Yes Minister' Made it Popular, but Does Winning a Nobel Prize Make it True?" *Canadian Public Administration* 31:1, pp. 12-26.

Borins, Sandford. 1998. *Innovating with Integrity: How Local Heroes are Transforming American Government.* Washington, D.C.: Georgetown University Press.

Borins, Sandford. 2001. *The Challenge of Innovating in Government.* Arlington, VA: IBM Endowment for the Business of Government. (www.businessofgovernment.org/pdfs/BorinsReport.pdf)

Brennan, Richard. 2000a. "Harris vows action on 407 'screw up'," *The Toronto Star*, February 24.

Brennan, Richard. 2000b. "Tolls on Highway 407 set to rise again May 1," *The Toronto Star*, April 14.

Canadian Council for Public-Private Partnerships. 2000. *National Awards Celebrating Innovation and Excellence: Case Studies of the 1999 Award Winning Projects for Infrastructure, Service Delivery, and Financing.* Toronto: Canadian Council for Public-Private Partnerships.

Cappe, Marni. 2004. "Breaking Gridblock – Lessons from London's Success Story," *Policy Options*, February, pp. 49-52.

Casella, Emilia. 1993. "Highway deal goes to NDP fundraisers," *The Hamilton Spectator*, April 18.

Clement, Barrie. 2004. "Suburban drivers to fall tolls in congestion charge shake-up," *The Independent*, January 2.

Corcoran, Terence. 1997. "Hwy. 407: the toll road that isn't," *The Globe and Mail*, July 23, p. B2.

Critchley, Barry. 1999. "Behind CHIC's $1 bid for 407," *The National Post*, April 15.

Crone, Greg. 1999. "Paving the drive to privatization," *The National Post*, April 15.

Daniels, Art and Scrivens, Brian.1997. "Taking Strategic Alliances to the World: Ontario's Teranet," pp. 235-45 in Ford, Robin and Zussman, David, *Alternative Service Delivery: Sharing Governance in Canada*. Toronto: Institute of Public Administration of Canada.

DeCloet, Derek. 2003. "To find SNC-Lavalin's hidden value, take the 407," *The Globe and Mail*, Dec. 4, p. B12.

Fell, Anthony. 2002. "Comments to the 10th Annual Conference on Public Private Partnerships," November 25. http://www.pppcouncil.ca/pdf/tonyfell.pdf.

Freeman, Alan, and Lewington, Jennifer. 2003. "All clear in central London," *The Globe and Mail*, March 1, p. A3.

General Accounting Office. 2004. *Private Sector Sponsorship of and Investment in Major Projects*, Report # GAO-04-419. Washington: General Accounting Office.

Girard, Daniel. 1999. "Ontario bags $3.1 billion from Highway 407 sale," *The Toronto Star*, April 14.

Globe and Mail. 2003. "Liberals told not to meddle with Highway 407 tolls," Nov. 30, p. A8.

Globe and Mail. 2004. "Stuck on Highway 407," July 13, p. A14.

Globerman, Steven and Vining, Aidan. 1996. "A framework for evaluating the government contracting-out decision with an application to information technology," *Public Administration Review* 56:6, pp. 577-87.

Gombu, Phinjo and Wilkes, Jim. 1997. "Fiasco of 407's flawed camera system," *The Toronto Star*, July 27, p. A1.

Hansard, 1994a. Proceedings of the Ontario Provincial Parliament, Question Period, April 18.

Hansard, 1994b. Proceedings of the Ontario Provincial Parliament, Question Period, April 19.

Hansard, 1994c. Proceedings of the Ontario Provincial Parliament, Question Period, April 25.

Hansard. 1996a. Proceedings of the Standing Committee on Estimates of the Ontario Provincial Parliament. February 13.

Hansard. 1996b. Proceedings of the Standing Committee on Public Accounts of the Ontario Provincial Parliament. October 17.

Hansard. 1996c. Proceedings of the Standing Committee on Public Accounts of the Ontario Provincial Parliament. November 21.

Hansard, 1998. Proceedings of the Resource Development Committee of the Ontario Provincial Parliament, November 19.

Hansard, 1999. Proceedings of the Ontario Provincial Parliament, Debates, May 4.

Hardin, Herschel. 1974. *A Nation Unaware: The Canadian Economic Culture.* Vancouver: J.J. Douglas.

Hutton, Will. 2003. "There's a lesson in London's triumph," *The Guardian (The Observer)*, March 2.

Ibbitson, John. 2000. "Highway sale helped pay for Tory campaign promises," *The Globe and Mail*, February 21, p. A19.

Ibbitson, John. 2004. "Highway tiff threatens Canada-EU trade deal," *The Globe and Mail*, August 11, pp. A1, A4.

Ingraham, Patricia, Joyce, Philip, and Donahue, Amy. 2003. *Government Performance: Why Management Matters*. Baltimore: Johns Hopkins.

Jacobs, Jane. 2004. *Dark Age Ahead*. Toronto: Random House Canada.

Kennedy, Randy. 2003. "The day the traffic disappeared," *The New York Times Magazine*, April 20, pp. 42-5.

Lewington, Jennifer and Campbell, Murray. 2004. "Deal for TTC derails threat of fare hike," *The Globe and Mail*, April 1.

Liberal Party of Canada. 2004. *Liberal Party Platform*, chapter 2, "Strengthening our Social Foundations." http://www.liberal.ca/platform_e_3.aspx

Lindgren, April. 1999. "Sale of the 407: the road ends, but will the toll?" *The National Post*, April 14, p. B2.

Lindgren, April. 2003. "Grits may backtrack on 407 tolls: 'Very complicated' contract with highway's owners may preclude reduction in usage fee," *The National Post*, December 2, p. A10.

Mackie, Richard. 2000. "System of private tollways under consideration, Eves says," *The Globe and Mail*, February 10, p.A19.

Mackie, Richard. 2004a. "Ontario considers toll superhighways to ease congestion," *The Globe and Mail*, March 12, p. A10.

Mackie, Richard. 2004b. "407 ETR sues to deny plate renewal for those who don't pay," *The Globe and Mail*, July 24, p. A9.

Mallan, Caroline. 2000. "Brakes go on 407 licence suspensions," *The Toronto Star*, February 25.

Ministry of Finance. 2000. *Annual Report: 1999-2000*. www.gov.on.ca/FIN/english/pacct/2000/00_are.htm

Ministry of Finance. 2004. 2004 *Ontario Budget: The Plan for Change*. www.ontariobudget.fin.gov.on.ca

Ministry of Public Infrastructure Renewal. 2004a. *Building a Better Tomorrow: Investing in Ontario's Infrastrcture to Deliver, Real, Positive Change.* http://www.pir.gov.on.ca/userfiles/HTML/cma_2_29245_1.html

Ministry of Public Infrastructure Renewal. 2004b. "New Infrastructure Framework – Financing Strategies," news release, July 27.

Ministry of Public Infrastructure Renewal. 2004c. *Places to Grow: A Growth Plan for the Greater Golden Horseshoe.* www.placestogrow.pir.gov.on.ca

Ministry of Transportation. 2000. "The Privatization of Highway 407," Presentation by the Strategic Projects Branch, October 17.

Ministry of Transportation. 2004a. "Ontario government serves 407 ETR with notice of default," news release, February 2.

Ministry of Transportation. 2004b. "Plate denial to remain suspended until 407 ETR meets requirements," news release, July 23.

Ministry of Transportation. 2004c. "Minister reiterates need to protect public," news release, July 30.

Mitchell, Bob. 1996a. "Police fear toll highway will be a killer: head-on crashes certain, they say," *The Toronto Star*, November 12, p. A1.

Mitchell, Bob. 1996b. "Highway 407 safety rules lowered: report," *The Toronto Star*, November 19, pp. A1, A24.

Mitchell, Bob. 1996c. "Province excluded in Highway 407 inspections: Contract with government lets builder do own," *The Toronto Star*, November 29, p. A7.

Mitchell, Bob. 1997a. "Highway 407 safety upgrades to cost up to $15 million: Province hopes toll road can open late May or early June," *The Toronto Star*, May 2, p. A2.

Mitchell, Bob. 1997b. "407 will remain free for now," *The Toronto Star*, July 6, p. A6.

Mitchell, Bob. 1997c. "40,000 cars a day could slip by 407 toll system: Province delays billing until extra computer set up," *The Toronto Star*, August 3, p. A7.

Mitchell, Bob. 1998. "Buyers will get to build costly extensions," *The Toronto Star*, February 21, p. A4.

Mylvaganam, Chandran. 1997. "Flying the User-Managed Skies: The Story of Nav Canada", in Robin Ford and David Zussman, *Alternative Service Delivery: Sharing Governance in Canada*. Toronto: Institute of Public Administration of Canada, pp. 223-31.

Office of Privatization. 1999. News release, May 5.

Organisation for Economic Cooperation and Development. 2001. "The Hidden Threat to E-Government" Paris: OECD PUMA Policy Brief No. 8 (www.oecd.org/puma/)

Palladini, Hon. Al, 1996. News release, December 20.

Parliamentary Office of Science and Technology. 2003. *Government IT projects*. www.parliament.uk/post

Perkins, Tara. 2003. "Highway 407 operator settles class action suit," *The Globe and Mail*, March 8, p.A21.

Pollitt, Christopher and Bouckaert, Geert. 2000. *Public Management Reform: A Comparative Analysis*. Oxford. Oxford University Press.

Premier of Ontario. 2004. "News Release: Renewing the Toronto Transit Commission – Governments Invest $1 Billion." March 30. www.premier.gov.on.ca/english/news/TTCInvestment033004.asp

Professional Engineers of Ontario. 1997a. "Highway 407 Safety Review Committee."

Professional Engineers of Ontario, 1997b. "News Release: Engineers Suggest Safety Modifications for Highway 407."

Provincial Auditor. 1996. *Annual Report.*

Reguly, Eric. 2004. "McGuinty & Co., your backdoor taxman." *The Globe and Mail*, July 13, p. B2.

Rogers, Everett. 1995. *Diffusion of Innovations.* 4th ed. New York: Free Press.

Smith, Graeme. 2002. "Taxpayers got good deal on sale of 407, Harris says," *The Globe and Mail*, January 10, p. A24.

SNC-Lavalin. 2002. *Reliability and Progress: 2002 Annual Report.* Montreal: SNC-Lavalin.

Teitel, Jay. 1998. "The road not taken," *Toronto Life*, November, pp. 73-87.

Toronto Star. 1999. Editorial: "Tolls forever," April 15.

Toronto Star. 2001. "Expansion plan in works for Highway 407," May 10.

Walker, William and Girard, Daniel. 1996. "Hwy 407 opening delayed to spring," *The Toronto Star*, November 21, pp. A1, A20.

Walkom, Thomas. 1994. Rae Days: *The Rise and Follies of the NDP.* Toronto. Key Porter Books.

Watson, Elizabeth. 2004. "Public-sector corporate governance: British Columbia's best-practices reforms," *Ivey Business Journal*, March-April, pp. 1-8.

Willis, Andrew. 2004. "407 ETR's battle with government taking toll on company," *The Globe and Mail*, July 14, p. A7.

Zussman, David. 2002. "Alternative Service Delivery", in Christopher Dunn, ed., *The Handbook of Canadian Public Administration.* Toronto: Oxford, pp. 53-76.

ENDNOTES

CHAPTER I

1 The only journalistic history of the Rae government (Walkom1994) made no mention of Highway 407.

CHAPTER 2

1 Several studies, in Europe primarily, have argued that while increasing highway capacity may alleviate congestion in the short term, it does not produce long-term relief. The growing influence of this view has been seen in the abandonment or scaling down in some European countries of plans for new highways. This view has not been generally adopted by decision-makers in Canada, or by the public at large, though it was one of the arguments adduced when the construction of the Spadina Freeway was halted in Toronto in the 1970s.

CHAPTER 3

1 The original line was "If you build it, he will come," referring to the legendary Chicago White Sox player Joe Jackson and featured in W.P. Kinsella's novel *Shoeless Joe*, published by Houghton Mifflin in 1982. The novel was subsequently filmed as *Field of Dreams*.

CHAPTER 4

1 The academic literature distinguishes between innovation, the adoption of an existing idea for the first time by a given organization, and invention, the creation of a new idea (Rogers 1995, 174-5). The first two features – faster construction and a design-build approach – are innovations in that they were being adopted for the first time in Ontario. The version of electronic tolling that was ultimately developed for Highway 407 – the integration of transponders for frequent users and videoimaging for occasional users – was rightly an invention, in that Highway 407 was the first in the world to develop this technology.

2 Mrs. Brown was Pouliot's example of the "average person" and, along with her cat Fluffy, regularly surfaced in the legislature and his ministerial office in relation to a variety of issues. He always wanted to know how policies would affect her and staff had to be prepared to respond beyond the broad policy questions. People who had

followed Pouliot's career were aware of the rich and varied lives that Mrs. Brown and Fluffy had led, entwined as they were in the vast range of issues that were dealt with by the Ontario government.

3   The City of Mississauga objected to the deferral of an interchange there and ultimately paid the incremental cost of reinstating it.

CHAPTER 6

1   Crown corporations had not been used in Ontario to oversee major highway projects. The New Democratic Party, however, tended to use Crown corporations for a wide range of economic interventions. The use of Crown corporations by the Saskatchewan NDP is discussed in Blakeney and Borins (1998).

2   The OFA was described in sections 29-37 of the Capital Investment Plan Act (Revised Statutes of Ontario 1993, chapter 23).

3   When George Davies and Jay Kaufman eventually left the OPS, their successors took their places on the board. Guscott later moved to Cabinet Office but remained on the board.

4   Professor Borins' views on road pricing, as expressed in his papers, could be characterized as agnostic. He had shown that, while tolls can lead to the optimal level of economic welfare (defined as the net present value of the difference between what users are willing to pay for a transportation system and the cost to society of producing it), the relative differences between the optimal policy and numerous sub-optimal policies are not great (Borins 1984). He also wrote a paper analyzing Hong Kong's 1985 experiment with electronic road pricing for the city centre (Borins 1988a). While the technology worked, the proposal was politically unpopular, primarily because of citizen concern regarding invasion of privacy in light of the impending handover of Hong Kong to China in 1997. As a result, it was not implemented. This experience led Professor Borins to suggest that electronic road pricing schemes might nowhere achieve sufficient public acceptance to be put in place.

5   The internal rate of return is the discount rate that produces a zero net present value for a project. In other words, it is the highest rate that the project can borrow at and still break even. In this case, as interest rates rose to 10%, the project's internal rate of return, it would no longer break even.

CHAPTER 7

1   Former NDP Transportation Minister Gilles Pouliot reminded the auditor that the government could borrow at a lower interest rate than the private sector, and Peters himself explained that, because the highway was intended to be self-financing, its construction costs

were being carried on the government's books as an asset (Hansard 1996b, 5,9).

2   At the same time, OTCC and the technology consortium signed an agreement of $3.9 million with Mark IV Industries to supply transponders.

3   Much of the computer software written in previous decades used only a two-space field for the year, with the consequence that the year 2000 (00) would be mis-read as 1900, potentially leading to widespread systems failures. Programmers who knew languages like COBOL in which these programs were written were in high demand to rewrite software before the end of 1999.

CHAPTER 8

1   Readers may be interested to known that Derech is the Hebrew word for road. "Derech Eretz" has the idiomatic meaning of "good behaviour," the implication being that a toll road will encourage Israel's normally aggressive drivers to be on their best behaviour.

2   The idea of tolling this highway was politically controversial in New Brunswick. After an election that resulted in a change of government, tolls were removed and the project became a simple design – build exercise.

3   It turned out that the budget was actually balanced in 1990-2000, with a small surplus of $688 million. Thus, the Conservatives were a year ahead of schedule on their deficit reduction plan. The $1.6 billion contribution from the net proceeds of the sale of Highway 407 was one of the key factors (Ministry of Finance 2000).

4   Grupo Ferrovial is 40% owned by Macquarie Infrastructure Group. Macquarie also directly purchased a 16% ownership share of 407 International from Caisse de depot et placement du Quebec. Grupo Ferrovial's subsidiary Cintra operates the highway, but Macquarie has effective financial control.

5   It should be noted that 407 International had a net loss of $97 million on revenues of $244 million in 2001, and a net loss of $99 million on revenues of $311 million in 2002. The reason for these accounting losses is that the highway incurs heavy depreciation and interest expenses in its early years. Cash flow is positive and the highway is already paying dividends. In its 2002 Annual Report, SNC-Lavalin's management included the following discussion of Highway 407:
"Highway 407 anticipates a trend of diminishing losses into future periods in order to progress towards a break-even point in earnings. As noted in prior years, SNC-Lavalin does not anticipate an accounting profit from its participation for the initial years of the 99-year concession. This is not unusual since highway concessions incur net accounting losses in the early years, mainly due to the high levels of

financing costs and depreciation expense. Positive cash flows generated from Highway 407, whereby the refinancing of the original debt was structured so as to match the expected revenues, have enabled 407 International Inc. to make dividend payments to investors despite accounting losses. Highway 407 paid SNC-Lavalin dividends totaling $11.8 million in 2002, which were only expected to be paid in 2003 based on the financial model used for this investment. Highway 407 expects to generate sufficient cash on a prospective basis to continue paying quarterly dividends" (SNC-Lavalin 2002, 43-44).

The market value of Highway 407 is based on expectations of future income and is consistent with accounting losses in the project's early years. The value of Highway 407 to SNC-Lavalin is also discussed in DeCloet (2003), and he draws a similar conclusion.

6   The pattern of political contributions during 2003 by 407 International and associated companies, including SNC Lavalin, as reported to Elections Ontario, makes interesting reading. During the first nine months of the year, they donated $24,150 to the Conservatives, who were still in office. The Liberals, who were doing extremely well in polls of voter preference, received $13,500 in the same period. The election took place on October 2. During the last three months of the year, essentially after the election, the successful Liberals received $55,100, while the Conservatives, who were now the opposition, received only $8,104. Clearly, however, 407 International's generosity towards the governing Liberals has not favourably influenced the government's decisions.

CHAPTER 9

1   The costs include the $53.4 million tolling system contract with the Bell/Bell Sygma/Hughes consortium, the $3.9 million transponder contract with Mark IV Industries, $15.5 million for cabling, $4.5 million for computer hardware for the billing system, all of which were budgeted, and the $13 million additional cost of increasing videoimaging capacity.

2   Whether net present value is a better criterion in general is a more complicated question. In projects whose output is not sold, using the net present value criterion would require an estimate of users' willingness to pay. If such measures can be developed, we would prefer the net present value criterion for measuring a project's success, at both the planning (ex ante) and evaluation (ex post) stages.

3   Interview, May 27, 2003.

4   Interview, May 23, 2003.

5   Given that the construction and tolling technology contracts were

between OTCC and the contractors, they were also available to OTCC directors and staff.

6   One gray area is awarding major contracts on the basis of regional economic impacts. In the case of Highway 407 procurement and privatization this was not a concern, because the proposals did not have differential regional impacts. In the case of major federal government contracts, the regional impacts may well be different, with the consequence that some politicians, particularly back-bench MPs, lobby on behalf of the regions they represent. In addition, it would no longer be possible for ministers to make a decision without knowing the names of the proponents, because any discussion of differential regional impacts would reveal the identity of the proposals that their back-bench colleagues, provincial governments, and regional media had all been touting.

7   Of course, every driver is the additional, or marginal, driver. If tolls were imposed, therefore, every driver would pay a fee representing the delay he or she imposes on other drivers.

8   One might also make a second best argument that, if there is no congestion pricing on highways and roads, government should subsidize public transit, even to the point where it is free. Again, such an argument would have economic validity, but it would lead to increased pressure on government spending. In Toronto, the capital costs of public transit are subsidized by the provincial and municipal governments, but fares have consistently been increased to cover rising operating costs and to make some contribution to capital costs. Of course, free transit could have the effect of taking drivers off the roads and putting them in buses and subway cars. The savings in road construction and maintenance could be funnelled to transit, resulting in environmental benefits as well.

9   The website, now defunct, carried the attention-getting URL www.millerhighwayrobbery.com.

10 The McGuinty government's conflict with 407 International has influenced its approach to the development of public infrastructure. A recent report states that "there must be appropriate safeguards against excessive financial returns where private financing is involved in the delivery of public infrastructure projects" (Ministry of Public Infrastructure Renewal 2004a, 12) and its accompanying background document, in discussing financing strategies, refers to "user fees, where appropriate and regulated" (Ministry of Public Infrastructure Renewal 2004b).

11 For example, if the government wanted to keep tolls low, it could accept zero return on its equity. That is, as debt is

retired, it would be converted to equity but no income would be imputed to that equity, just as is the case with owner-occupied housing.

12 The sceptical interpretation about the motives of politicians and public servants derives from public choice theory, which assumes that a politician's primary goal is winning the next election and a public servant's primary goal is building his/her bureaucratic empire (Borins 1988b).

13 A recent study assessing public management performance in the United States argues that non-recurring revenues should not be used to finance continuing expenditures "because this can mean that government will find it more difficult to finance its expenses in subsequent years" (Ingraham, Joyce, and Donahue 2003, p. 34). This would imply using revenues from the sale of Highway 407 to retire debt rather than contribute to the current budget. In Canada, however, governments have generally used non-recurring revenues to support the current budget.

ACKNOWLEDGMENTS

We have known one another for quite some time, and the book had its genesis in our friendship. While studying for his MBA at York University in 1989, Chandran Mylvaganam attended the public management course taught by Sandford Borins and Allan Blakeney, former premier of Saskatchewan. Shortly after Mylvaganam completed his MBA in 1990, the NDP was elected in Ontario. Mylvaganam left his position at Ontario Hydro to become chief of staff to the Minister of Transportation, a position he held under three ministers – Ed Philip, Gilles Pouliot and Mike Farnan – until the NDP was defeated in 1995. Borins was nominated to the board of the Ontario Transportation Capital Corporation in May 1995 by Premier Rae and served a three-year term. Mylvaganam was involved in one of the unsuccessful bids for the privatization of Highway 407 in 1998-99. We have been friends since our association in the York MBA program and one of our topics of appropriately discreet conversation has been Highway 407.

After the privatization of Highway 407 and ensuing controversies, we both came to feel that the true story of Highway 407 was not well known. Initially, we thought we could tell it in the confines of an academic paper. We soon realized it would require a book, and this is the product of that realization.

We have several people and institutions to thank for their contribution. Several current and former Ontario public servants agreed to be interviewed, and a few read drafts. We also interviewed key figures associated with the private sector consortia that participated in the development and privatization competitions. Our capable research assistants included Danielle Katic, Milica Uzelac, and Li Zhou. Jowenne Herrera produced the imaginative cover design, map, and table. Pauline Harnum ably organized the production and distribution of copies of drafts of the manuscript. Barbara Schon prepared a comprehensive index. Janet Slavin ably oversaw the production process. Beth Herst copy-edited the penultimate draft, and offered many helpful suggestions. The manuscript was reviewed by Professor Andrew Stark, editor of the series, and two anonymous reviewers, all of whom made many helpful suggestions. Our research expenses were covered by the Division of Management of the University of Toronto at Scarborough.

Sandford Borins spent the 2003-04 academic year on leave from the university as Scholar in Residence in the Cabinet Office of the Ontario Government, which proved to be a supportive environment for completing the project. The views expressed in this book, however, are entirely those of the authors and do not reflect those of the Cabinet Office nor the current or former Governments of Ontario.

ACKNOWLEDGMENTS

INDEX

dates, 74
Currie, Paul, 74
customer service, 96–99

Davies, George, 36, 56, 111–12, 148n. 3(6); contract award announcement, 42; deputy minister of transportation, 18–19, 110; director OTCC, 58–59; and MTO, 20–21, 25; and post-award briefing, 116; and proposal review committee, 31; replacement of by Rush, 63; tolling consortium, 34, 50; tolling contracts, 70
decision-making: approach to, 19–20; Rae government, 111
Delcan Associates, 24, 59, 122
Deloitte & Touche, 101
Development, Design, Build Agreement, 48
Dillon Consulting, 76
Don Valley Parkway, road tolls, 120
Durham region, 22

East Don river, 24
economics, theory of the second best, 119
Elections Canada, political contributions 2003, 150n. 6(8)
election 1995, 53
election 1999, 75; campaign, 124; pre-election revenues, 85–87
election 2003, toll levels on 407, 99
Electricians Union, 35
electronic tolling systems, 2–4, 34–35, 40–41, 43; 400-series highways, 131; central cities, 131; invention, 147n. 1(4). *See also* road tolls
electronic tolling technologies, 16, 69–72, 108; London, England, 120

employment equity, 58, 111
engineering industry, design/build projects, 13–14
Environmental Assessment Act, 79
environmental groups, 23–24
evaluation: IT-based project, 106–7; process, 32–33; of proposals, 31–36, 39–41
Eves, Ernie, 74; chair of CCOP, 84; need for pre-election revenues, 85–86
Eves government: legacy of, 104; privatization contract, 117; sale of Teranet, 128; toll rate agreements, 95
expansion, 94–96
expression of interest (EOI), 76
external directors, OTCC, 76, 112–13, 130

fairness issues, 115–18; contracting process, 48
Farnan, Mike: appointment of to Transportation, 50; and sole-sourcing contract to ORDC, 51–52; western section of Highway 407, 52
federal government, privatization, 2
fees and penalties, 96–99
Fell, Anthony, 93
finance: balanced budget 1990-2000, 149n. 3(8); deficit reduction plan, 89; financial advisors, 21; non-recurring revenues and current budgets, 152n. 13(9)
financing: borrowing, 62; capital projects, 12; construction, 8; debt financing, 40; fiscal impact on province, 33; highways, 15; Highway 407, 16, 61–62; loans from OFA, 61; off-book, 12–13; Ontario Hydro, 62; public, 39–40;

Markham Road. *See* Highway 48
Mark IV Industries, 35: agreement to supply transponders, 69, 149n. 2(7)
Marshall Macklin Monaghan (MMM), 14, 24
media, and licence plate denial, 97
Merrill Lynch, 75
Michals, George, director OTCC, 58
Miller, David, 120–21
Ministry of Economic Development and Trade (MEDT), 25
Ministry of Finance: opposition from, 56–57; toll highway, 19
Ministry of Northern Development, northern highways program, 9
Mississauga, interchange deferral, 148n. 3(5)
Mitchell, Bob, 65–66
Morrison Hershfield, 51
MTO (Ministry of Transportation), 27–28; appointment of deputy minister, 18; capital budgeting, 8–9; competitive tendering process, 52; dissatisfaction within, 20–21; eastern extension of 407, 50–51; as economic development ministry, 20; enforcement of penalties, 88–89; and opposition of, 17; and OTCC, 57; project development, 17–18, 21, 26; Quality and Standards Division, 19; road construction supervision, 10; role of, 110; and sole-sourcing contract, 51–52; toll roads, 15, 16
Mulroney government, Confederation Bridge (PEI), 21
municipalities, and MTO, 10

NAFTA, external competition, 11
Nav Canada, 2
NDP Government: OTCC mandate under, 114; procurement process, 116-18; tolling policy, 121. See also New Democratic Party (NDP)
net present value, Highway 407, 108, 150n. 2(9)
New Brunswick, tolling in, 149n. 2(8)
Newcourt Credit, 77
New Democratic Party (NDP), 110; difference between Conservatives and, 63; fundraising dinner, 38–39, 45–46; and road construction industry, 11; support within party, 24; user pay philosophies, 26. *See also* NDP Government
Newmarket, 6
99-year lease, 80–81, 87–88; and 1999 election platform, viii; Privatization Secretariat, 81; unprecedented lease period, 104
Norontair, 75
Nova Scotia, Highway 104, 77

Office of Privatization. *See* Privatization Secretariat
OMERS, 77
Ontario Financing Authority (OFA), 56, 61–62
Ontario Hydro, 13–14, 74
Ontario Motor Coach Association, 23
Ontario Provincial Police (OPP), 65–68; policing services, 89
Ontario Public Service Employees' Union (OPSEU), highway inspectors, 66
Ontario Public Service (OPS), 56, 58, 114
Ontario Realty Corporation, 63
Ontario Road Builders Association, 23

Ontario Road Development Corporation. *See* ORDC (Ontario Road Development Corporation)

Ontario Superior Court, dispute resolution, 99

Ontario Transportation Capital Corporation (OTCC), 3–4, 43, 78, 81; average cost of borrowing, 62; contract award announcement, 42–43; Crown corporation, 55–56; decision-making of, 36; divesting of, 127; external directors, 57–58, 75, 112–13, 130; financing, 61; marketing campaign, 64; operations, 60–61; penalties to, 108; powers of, 57; privatization, 75–77; project management, 112–15, 129–30; risk management, 69; scenario as a Crown corporation, 128–29; staff increases at, 59; turnover of Highway 407, 90; weaknesses of, 113

Ontario Trucking Association, 23

Operating Engineers Union, 23

ORDC (Ontario Road Development Corporation), 24, 25, 77; bid, 84; consortium, 26–27, 35; and contract award briefing, 43; eastern extension of 407, 50–51; l consortium, 116; NDP fundraising dinner, 39; and post-award briefing, 116; proposal, 36; reaction of, 43–44, 47–48; RFQ, 29

Organisation for Economic Co-operation and Development (OECD): on managing major IT projects, 114–15; on managing public sector IT projects, 106

Oshawa, 6

Oshawa-Clarington border, 79

outsourcing, 21

Palladini, Al, 108; marketing the highway, 112; safety issues, 66–68, 71

Parkway Belt lands, property acquisition, 6

Parsons Brinkerhoff, 76

Patterson, Dale, 51

Pearson, Bill, 46

Pearson International Airport: process, 47; redevelopment controversies, 21; Terminal 3, 14

penalties, for non-payment of tolls, 96–99

Peter Kiewit Sons, 29, 77

Peters, Erik, 64–67, 148–49n. 1(7)

Peterson, David, 7, 11

Petrocan, viii

Phillips, Gerry, 46

photo billing, 41

Policy and Priorities Board (P&P), 19–20; approvals for highway extensions, 51; Capital Investment Plan Act, 56–57; competitive tendering process, 52; and decision to proceed, 22; direction from, 36–38; objectives, 26, 37; partnerships, 26; policy recommendations, 39–41; proposal review committee, 31–32, 36, 39

politics: contract award reaction, 44–45; decision-making by politicians, 82; of highway expansion, 8; of Highway 407, 63–67, 111; minimizing political involvement, 21–22; and the 905 area, 97–98; northern highways program, 9; regional impacts and, 151n. 6(9); and road construction industry, 10–11

Posen, Gary, 18–19

Pouliot, Gilles, 13, 16, 25, 34, 110,

request for proposals (RFP), 28, 30, 35, 78–80

request for qualifications (RFQ), 25, 27, 29

Research Enterprises Limited, 127

revenues, 108; gasoline tax, 131

risk assessment, 32; monitored by OTCC, 69–70

risk management: monitored by OTCC, 69; OTCC, 113

road construction industry, 10–11

road pricing, 148n. 4(6); London, England, 120; and public transit argument, 151n. 8(9); to reduce urban sprawl, 120. *See also* toll roads

road tolls, vii, 120–24; appropriateness of, 118–24; arguments over, 118–24; enabling, 130–31; increases in, 99, 103; penalties for non-payment, 88–89; principles of, 27; sale of concession, 92; and transit funding, 121; unpaid, 101. *See also* electronic tolling systems

Royal Bank of Canada (RBC), 91

Rush, Jan, 111–12; appointment of as deputy minister of transportation, 63; tolling contracts, 70–71

safety, 64–69, 71, 108, 111

Salerno, Tony, 14, 31, 46, 56, 59, 81

SAMCI (formerly Susan A. Murray Consulting Inc.), 33

Sampson, Rob, 74, 75, 89, 94, 103; Bill 70, 78; and Privatization Secretariat, 76–77

Santa Monica Freeway, 6

Scott, J. Michael, 58

Shoeless Joe (Kinsella), 16, 147n. 1(3)

Sirit Technologies, 35–36, 43

Skydome, 37

SNC-Lavalin, 77, 92, 129; political contributions 2003, 150n. 6(8); and shares of 407 International, 126; value of 407 International to, 149–50n. 5(8)

Southam chain, 45

Spadina Freeway, 147n. 1(2)

Spain: toll roads, 14–15; Trade and Investment Agreement between Canada and the European Union, 102

stakeholders, 17–18, 22–24

Standard and Poor, value of highway (2003), 92

Standish Group, 106, 108–9

steering committee, 81–83

Stewart, Barbara, 56–57

Stockwell, Chris, 46

subways. *See* public transit

Takhar, Harinder, 100–101

Tanenbaum, Larry, 24, 43, 51

task complexity, 106–7

Taylor, Alex, 25

TD Bank, 77

Teamsters Union, 23, 35

technology consortium, 69–72; monitored by OTCC, 70; shortage of COBOL programmers, 71

Teitel, Jay, 118–19

Teranet, 36–37, 127–28

Thomson family, 77

Tolling, Congestion Relief and Expansion Agreement, 94–96

tolling consortium, three-way agreement, 50

tolling partners, 34–35

tolling technology, 28–29, 32, 88, 111; contract deadlines, 70–71; cost of, 108, 150n. 1(9); leading-edge development, 71

toll rates, 32, 88, 94–96, 107–8; cabinet approval of, 41; contract governing, 94; increases in, 94; parameters, 95; setting, 83; since privatization, 121–24; standard value for, 95. *See also* road tolls

toll roads, vii, 24, 72, 77; 407 highway, 15, 54, 72; free use period of Highway 407, 71–72; and MTO, 15; Ontario, 15; West European countries, 14–15

toll threshold, 95

Toronto: road tolls, 120; subway lines in, 18

Toronto Life, 118

The Toronto Star, 65, 66–67, 90

Toronto Stock Exchange, 42

Toronto Transit Commission (TTC), 120–21

Tory, John, 120

traffic congestion, 88, 107; cost of in the GTA, 7; as election issue, 7; relief, 94–96; social cost of, 119

traffic threshold, growth index, 95

traffic volumes, 83; agreement, 96; area of dispute, 100–101; growth of, 73; measurement of, 95

transit. See public transit

transparency issues, 115–18

transponders: issues, 28–29; usage, 101; and videoimaging technologies, vii, 69

transportation: infrastructure, 1–2, 15; priorities, 18

Transport Canada, 14

Treasury Board, 25

trucking industry: and the automobile industry, 7; reaction of to a toll highway, 60

Turnbull, David, 46–47, 53, 95, 98

TV Ontario, 74

United Kingdom: Next Step agencies,
61; Parliamentary Office of Science and Technology, 106, 110

United States: Highway 401 corridor and, 6; toll roads, 15

urban sprawl, 119

urban transportation policy, 3

U.S.-Canada free trade agreement, external competition, 11

user pay concept, 26, 28

value: concession to toll, 92; extension to Brock Road, 83–84; of Highway 407, viii, 92–93, 149–50n. 5(8)

value engineering, 27, 29–30; appraisal of, 32; savings from, 64

vehicle registration, denial of, 96

vehicles, out-of-province, 41

videoimaging technology, 88; processing problems, 70; and transponder technologies, 69

video plate capture, 41

Vining, Aidan, 106

Warren Paving, 24, 77

Weppler, Murray, 42

Whitby, 22

Wilbur Smith Associates (WSA), 21, 76; traffic modelling, 122, 124

Windsor, 6

Wolfson, Judith, 36–37, 82

Wood, Bob, 75

Woodbridge Company, 77, 84–87, 125–26

Woodbridge Company consortium, Royal Bank of Canada, 91

Zimmerman, Richard, 60